My Yorkshire Sketchbook

Ashley Jackson

Dalesman

First published in 2012 by Dalesman
an imprint of
Country Publications Ltd
The Water Mill, Broughton Hall
Skipton, North Yorkshire BD23 3AG
www.dalesman.co.uk

ISBN 978-1-85568-309-9

Printed in China by 1010 Printing.

Endpapers: a closeup of Ashley's painting smock.

Dedication: I dedicate this book to my daughter Claudia who has been influential in inspiring me to open my personal sketchbooks, revisit the past memories and then assisted in putting these thoughts and feelings in to words. I also wish to thank Yorkshire for continuing to inspire me; my passion for you has deepened over the years like a true love affair, I hope to never waken without that longing in my heart.

These drawings from my personal sketchbooks are my love letters from Mother Nature. They haven't been spruced up; they are the raw sketches done at lightning speed to capture that moment in time.

The feelings remain long after the initial essence has been bottled. Like life's elixir, you can then come back and uncork the bottle when ever you feel.

I would say to any artist: never work from photographs; take a small sketchbook and pencil with you where ever you travel, it allows you to capture so much more than just an image ... thoughts, feelings, the weather and most importantly where the light is coming from — for without light there is no shade and no depth to your painting. Remember that, throughout this book, the arrows on the sketches depict the direction of light, and will help you visualise the light and shade within the original location.

Age and time have not withered or diminished this love affair I have with my Yorkshire mistress. I feel an infinite pull to stand on the moors and gaze at her beauty and contours, but just like a woman she has moods of tenderness and passion.

Looking back through past sketchbooks provided me with the passionate words of a young artist back in 1971, setting off with portfolio in hand:

Yorkshire, if not for you I would
not be an artist.
You are the one who made
My eyes see and my heart feel.
Friends will leave, but you
will stay long after my
days have gone.
It's your soul and
only yours that keeps
me sane!
if I lost my eyes I would
Keep you in My soul"

Ashley Jackson 1971

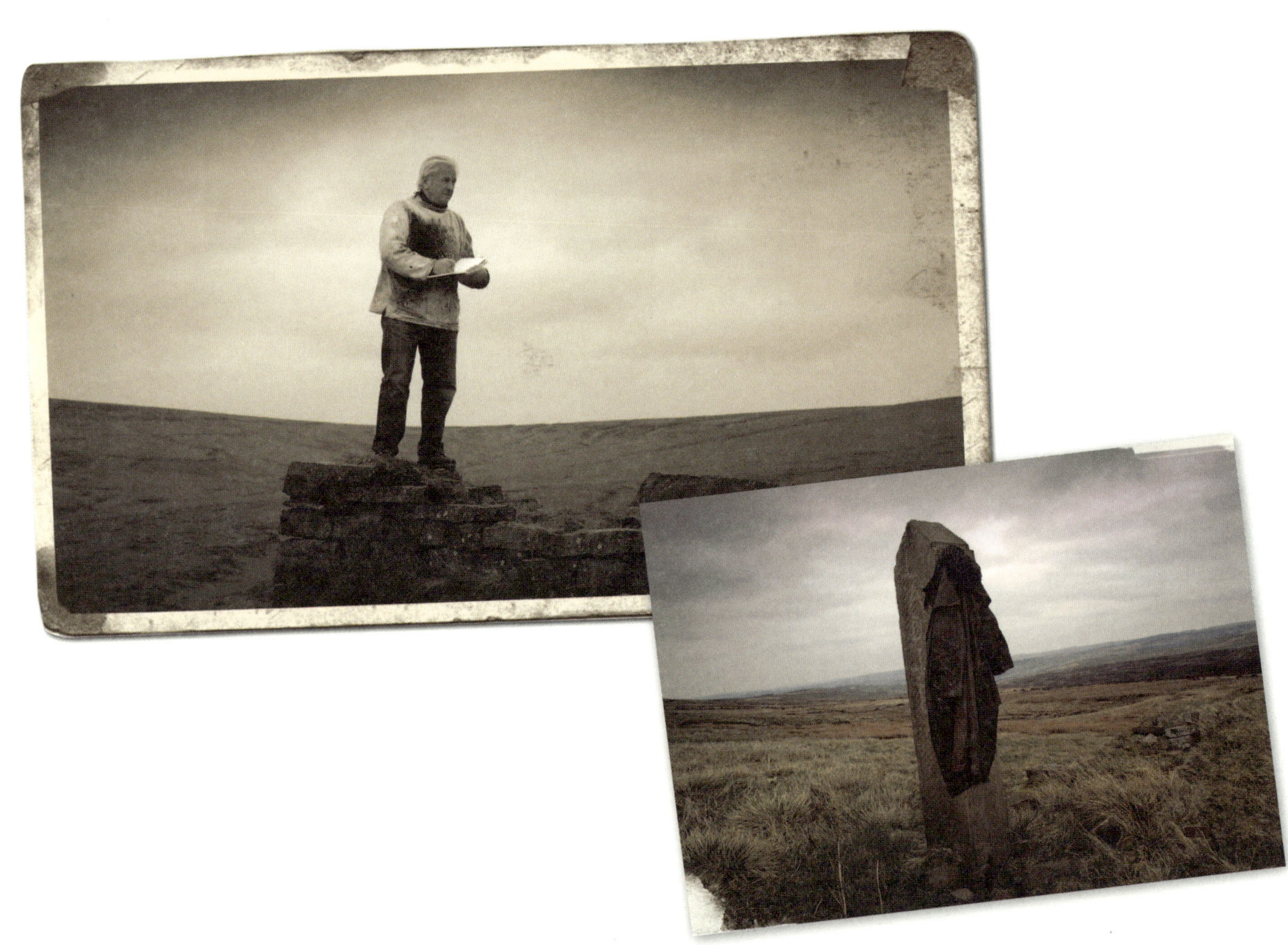

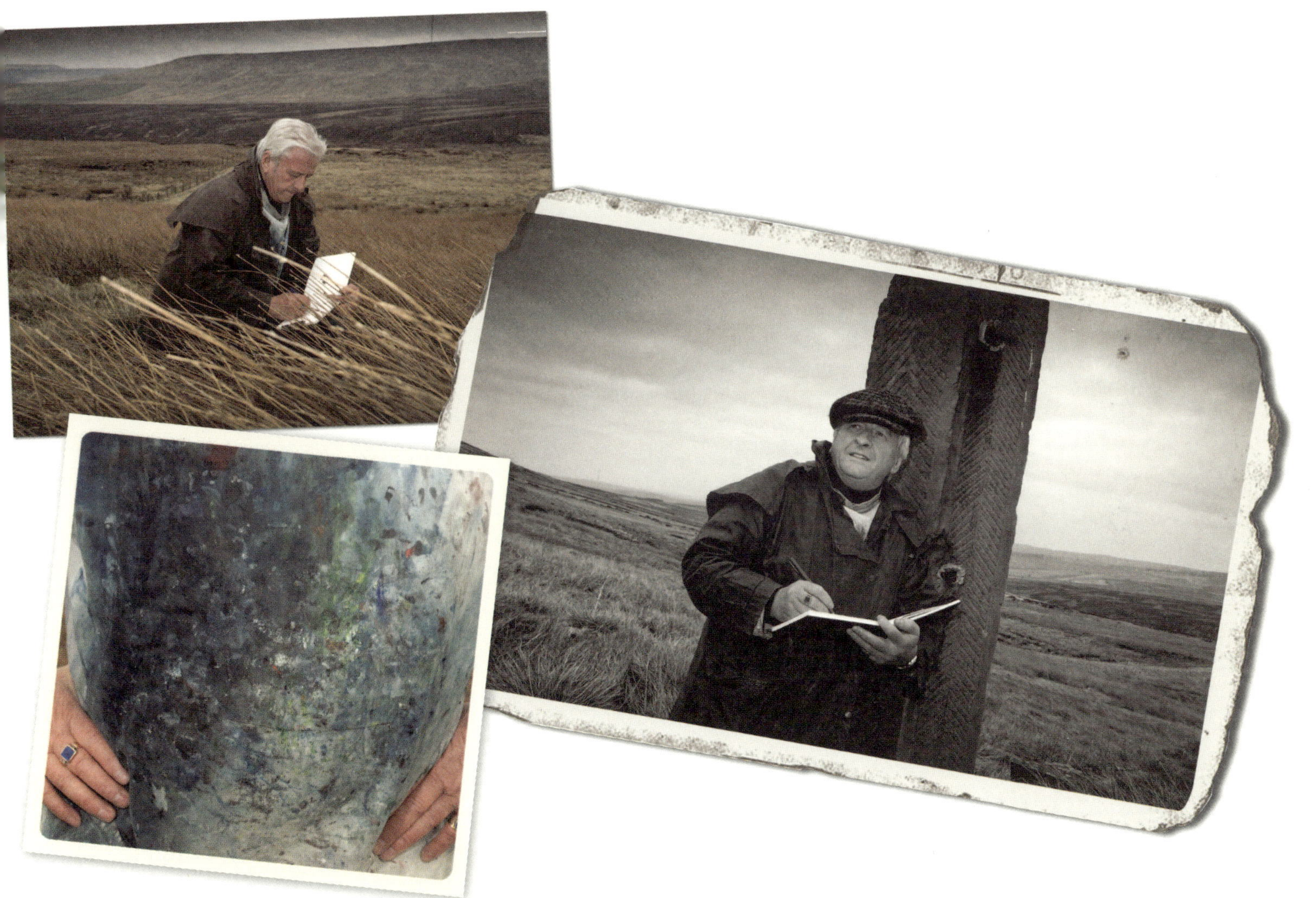

Tan Hill

Many years ago I painted Tan Hill; this painting became a limited edition which I believe is still hung in the inn today. The painting was long before double glazing was installed at the pub, but even then its hospitality was renowned for accommodating the travellers utilising the old packhorse road. The sketch is where the Yorkshire moors look into Teesdale – it is Yorkshire at its highest point. The arrows depict where the light is coming from.

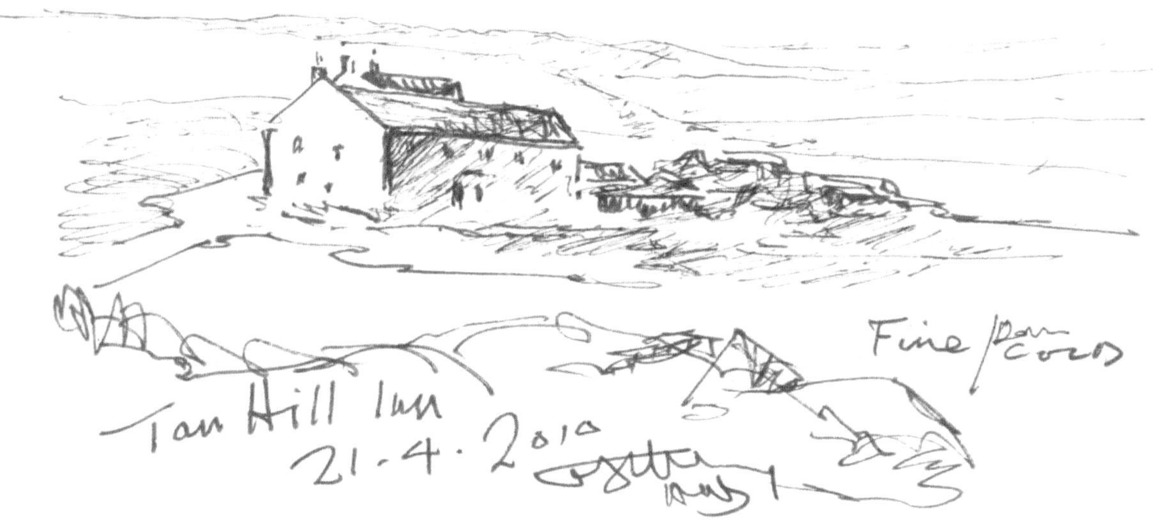

Arkengarthdale

This is one of the most remote northern dales and a tributary valley of Swaledale. It was once the home of a thriving leadmining industry. The sketch is of the route to Tan Hill from Reeth. It was a fine day with the clouds/shadows sweeping across the moor.

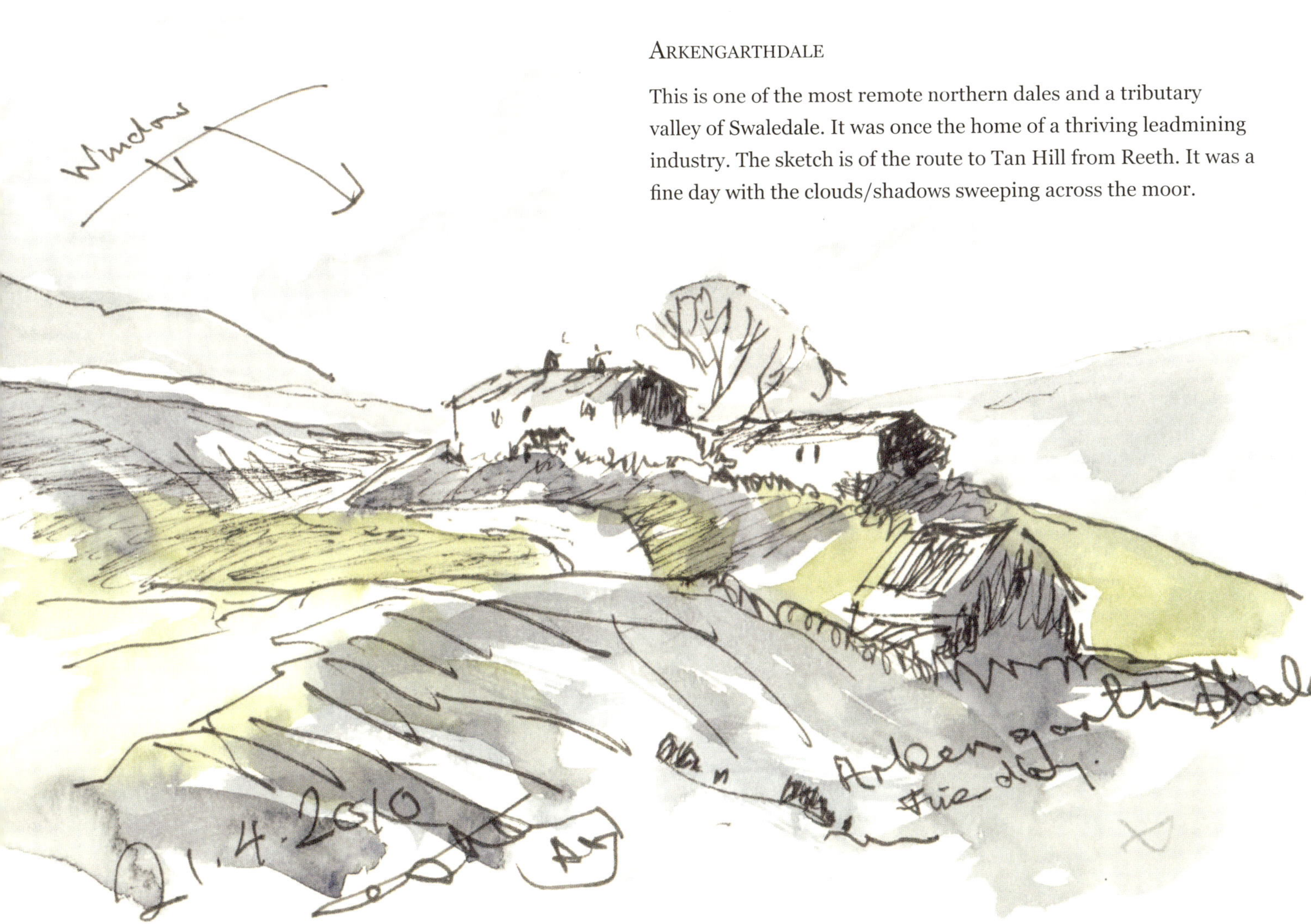

The Lion Inn, Blakey

Blakey Ridge with the Lion in the background is a favourite stop-over for hikers doing the Lyke Wake Walk. Way upon the ancient burial grounds these druid stones stand, like fingers piercing the sky, telling you 'I told you so'. This finished painting is a favourite of mine and was first exhibited at the Power and the Passion exhibition at the Mall Galleries, London, as a celebration of my seventieth birthday and continued love-affair with Yorkshire.

I have added the colour painting so that you may get a depth of the view that captured my inspiration that day.

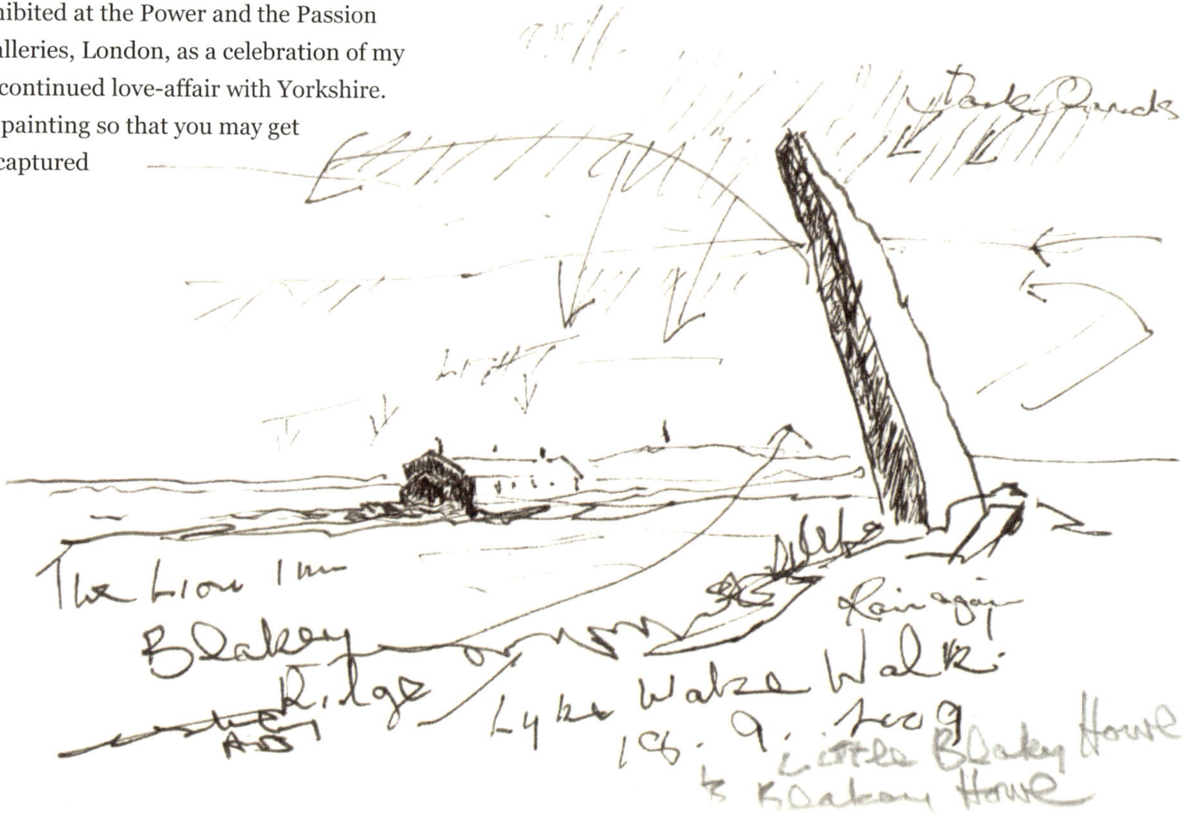

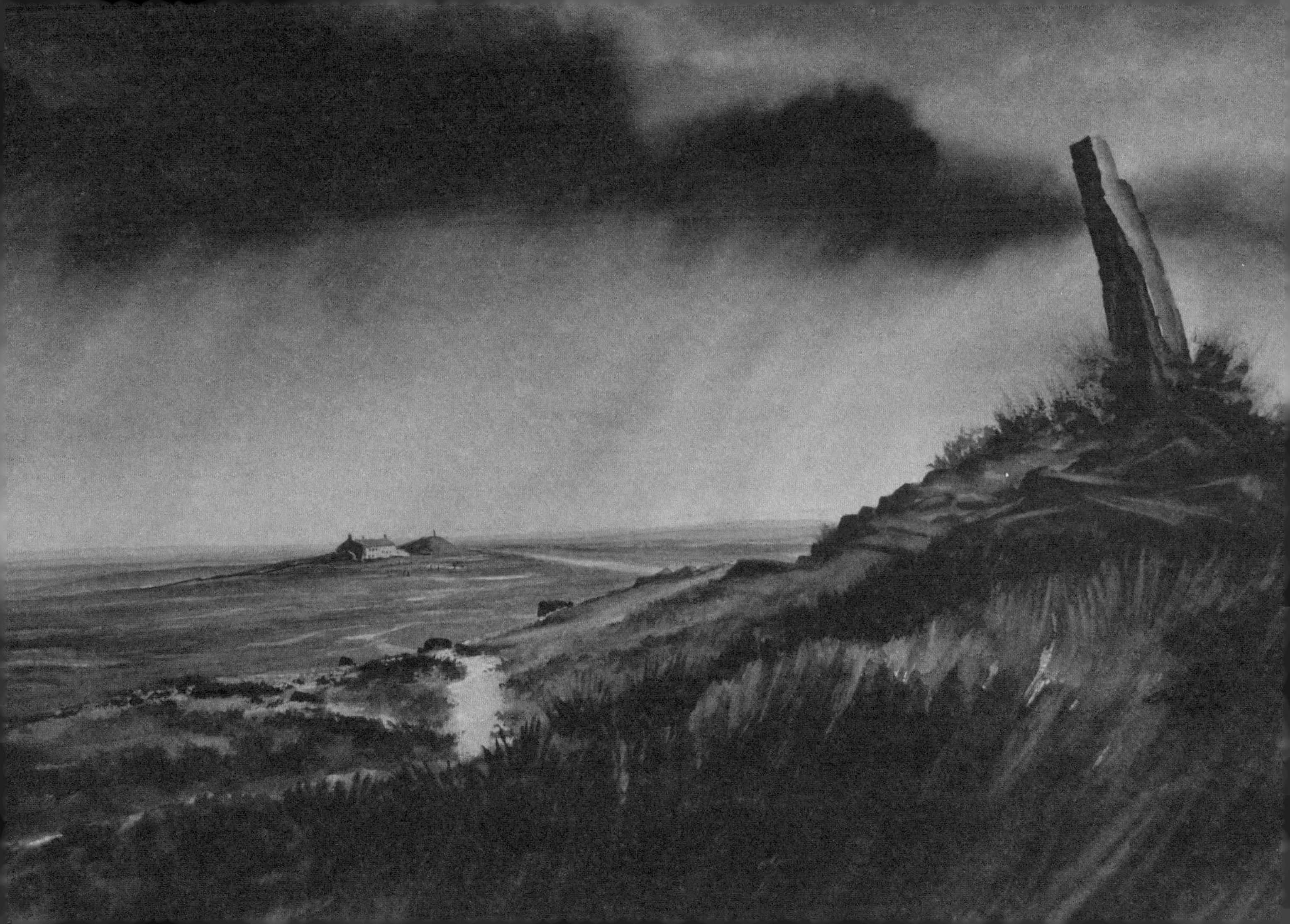

Robin Hood's Bay

An artist's paradise for a coastal scene. Park your car at the top of the steep cliff and walk down the cobbles. The houses hang on to the cliff edge, making a dramatic sight. Another cove that compares to the drama of Robin Hood's Bay is Runswick Bay nearby.

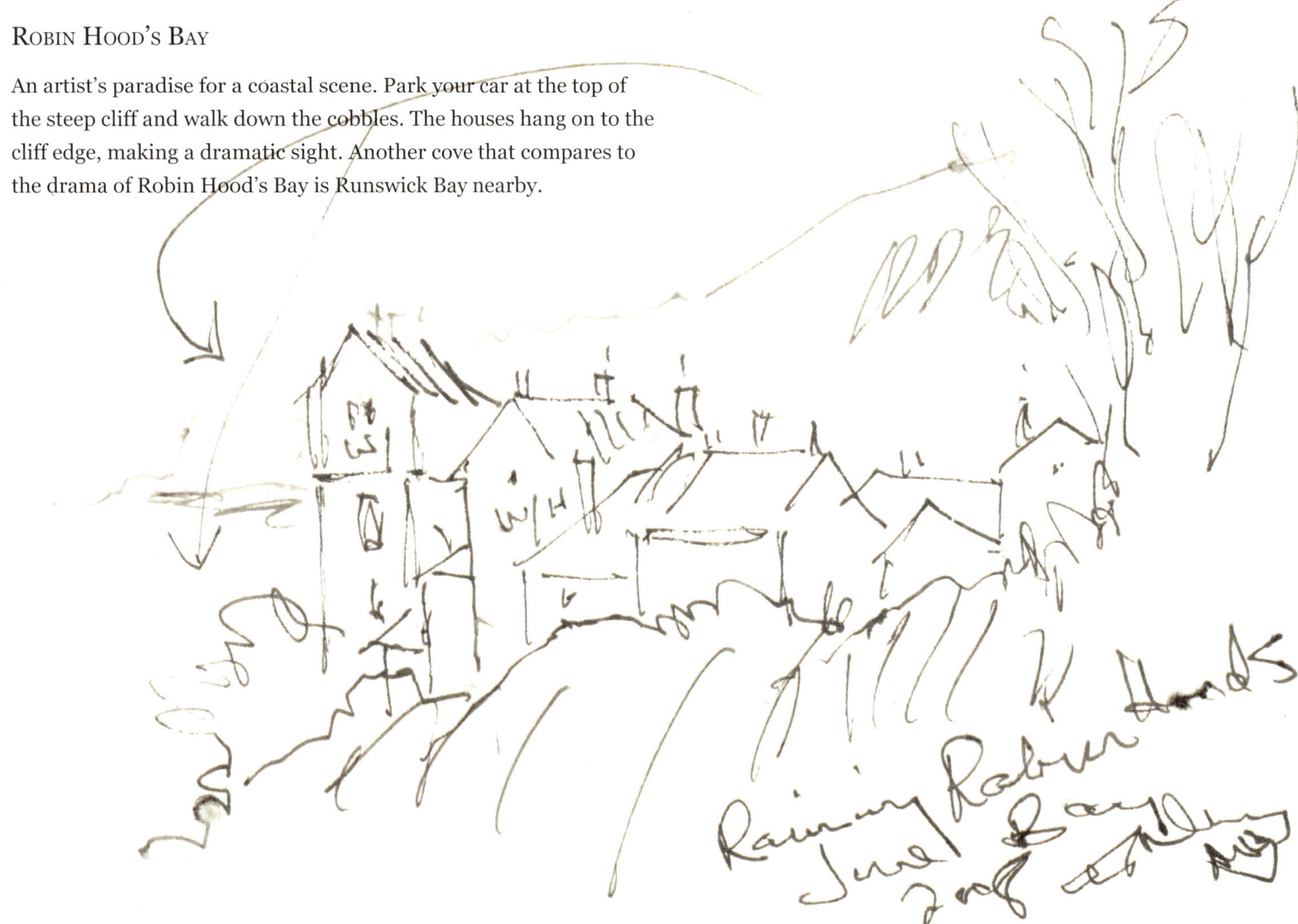

I was so fascinated by the bay I chose to stay a while and capture three different sketches, all from slightly different angles.

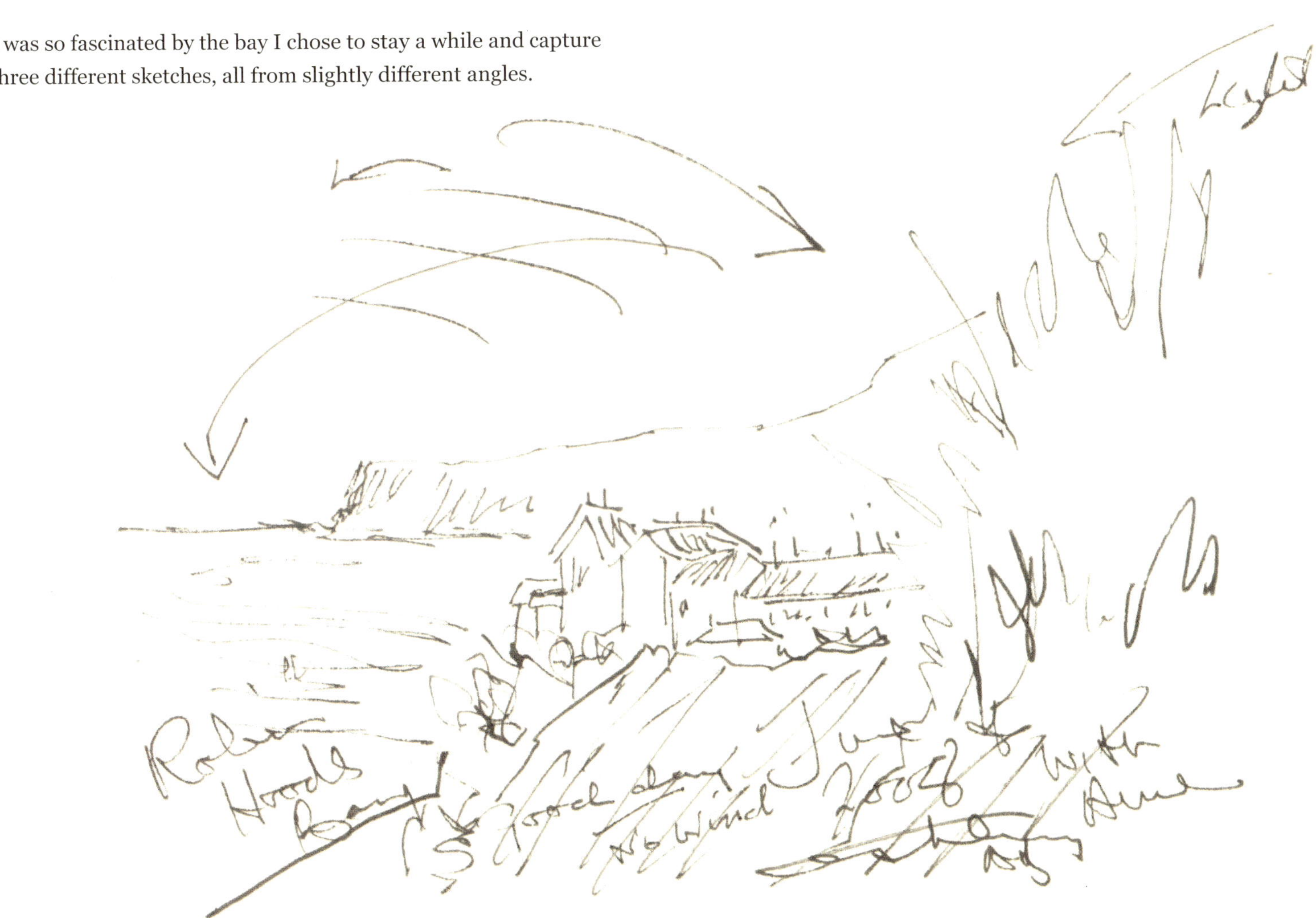

To create the jewel of the cove I had to go across two pages in my sketchbook with a quick watercolour sketch. On a windswept day, smelling the salty air was a real tonic.

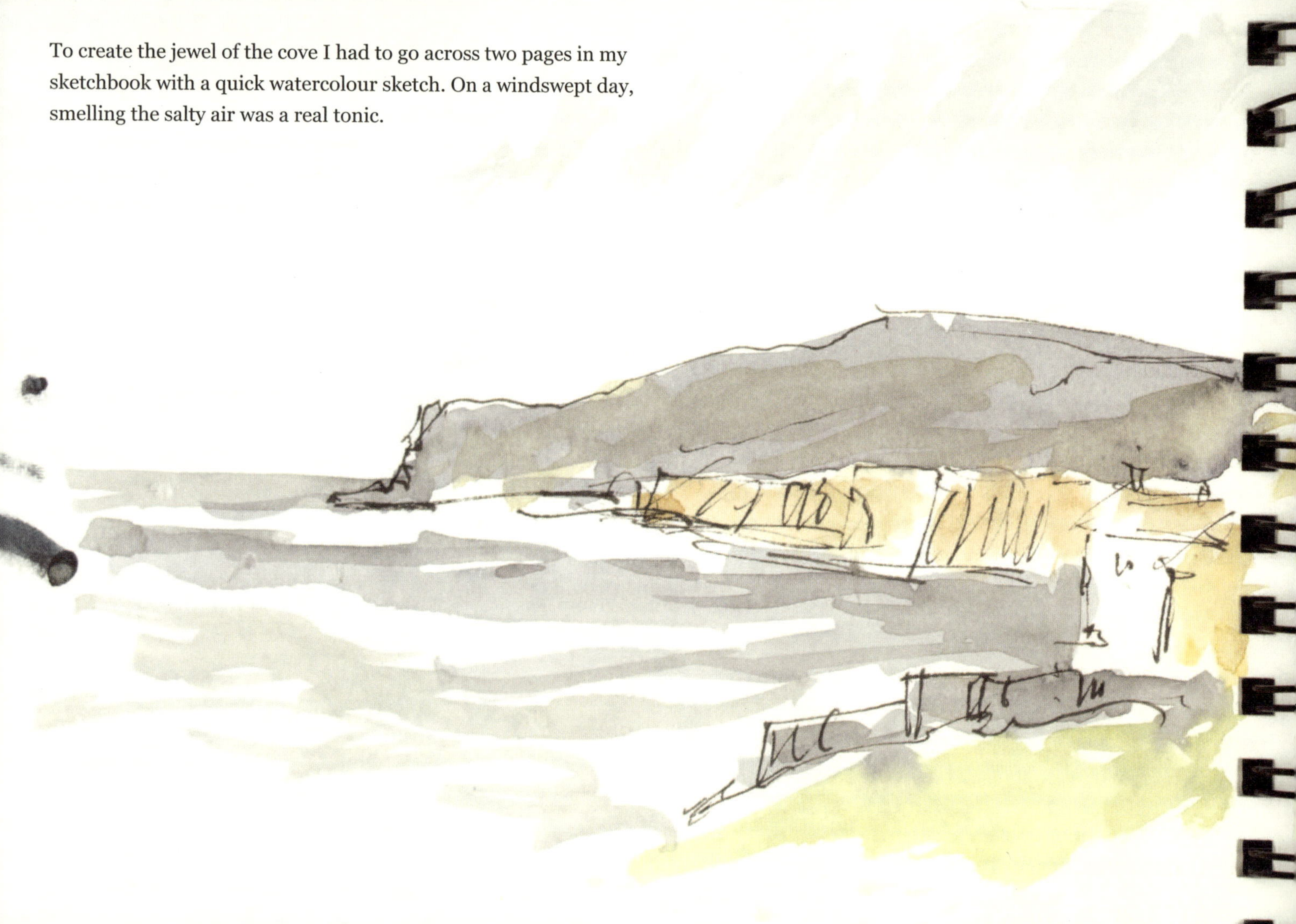

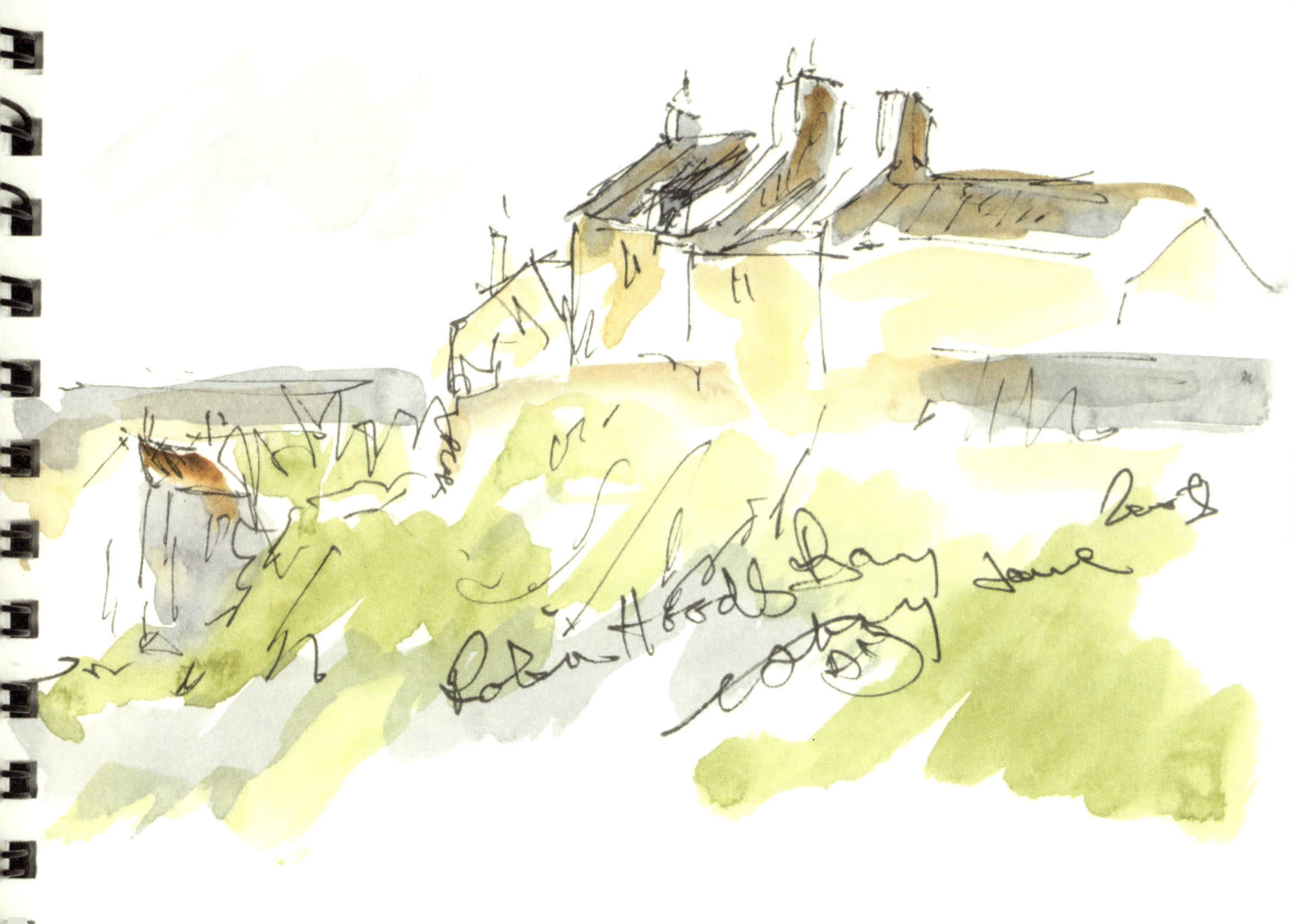
Robin Hood's Bay

Little Blakey Howe

I completed the Lyke Wake Walk in 1963 when I was twenty-two, with a group of friends from Barnsley. To be a 'dirger' you had to achieve forty miles over the open moors with just map and compass within twenty-four hours. I still believe that it was measured by vultures waiting to pick you off across the moor rather than 'as the crow flies'. No matter how dark the day is, there is always a break of heavenly light which gives me faith.

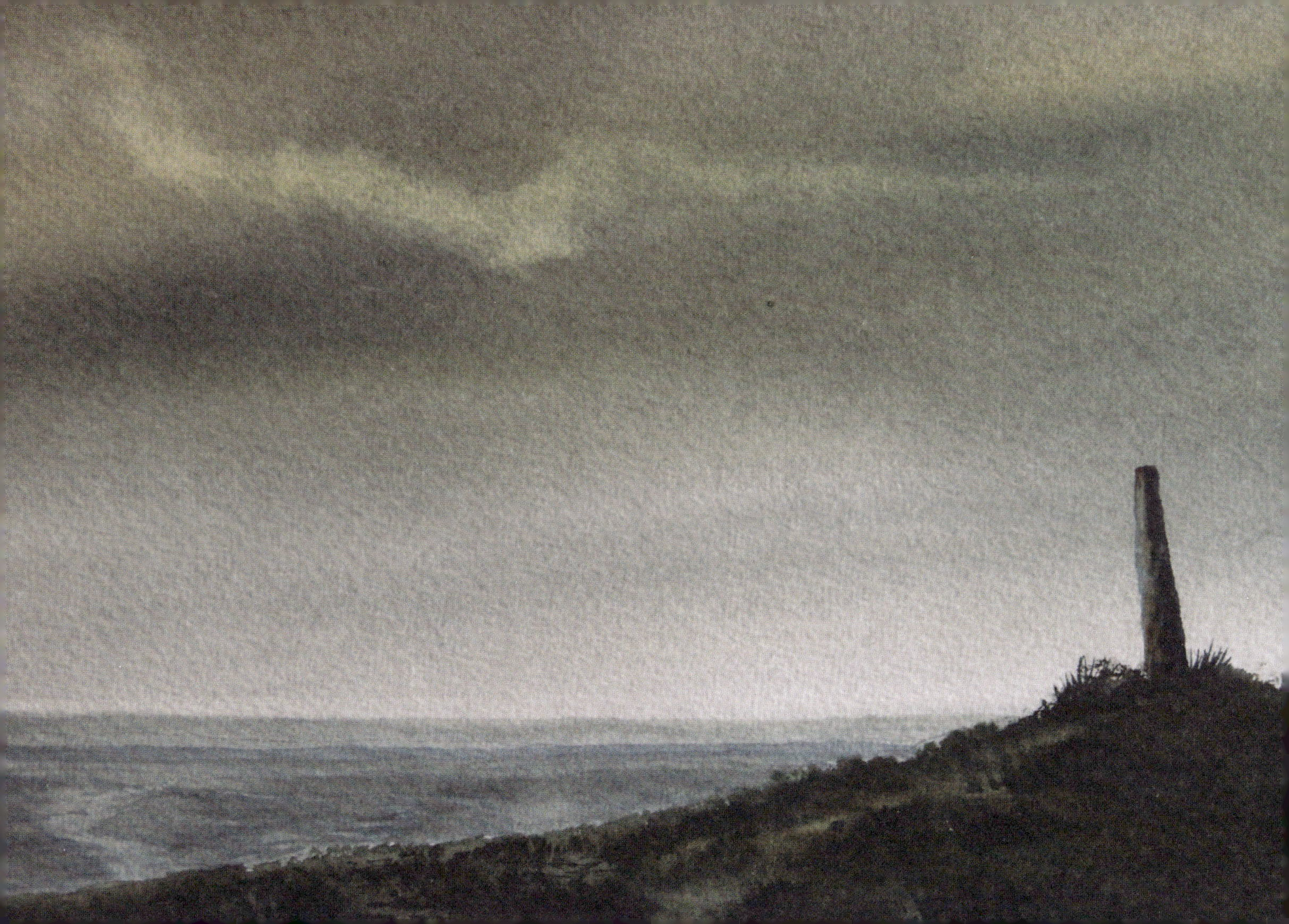

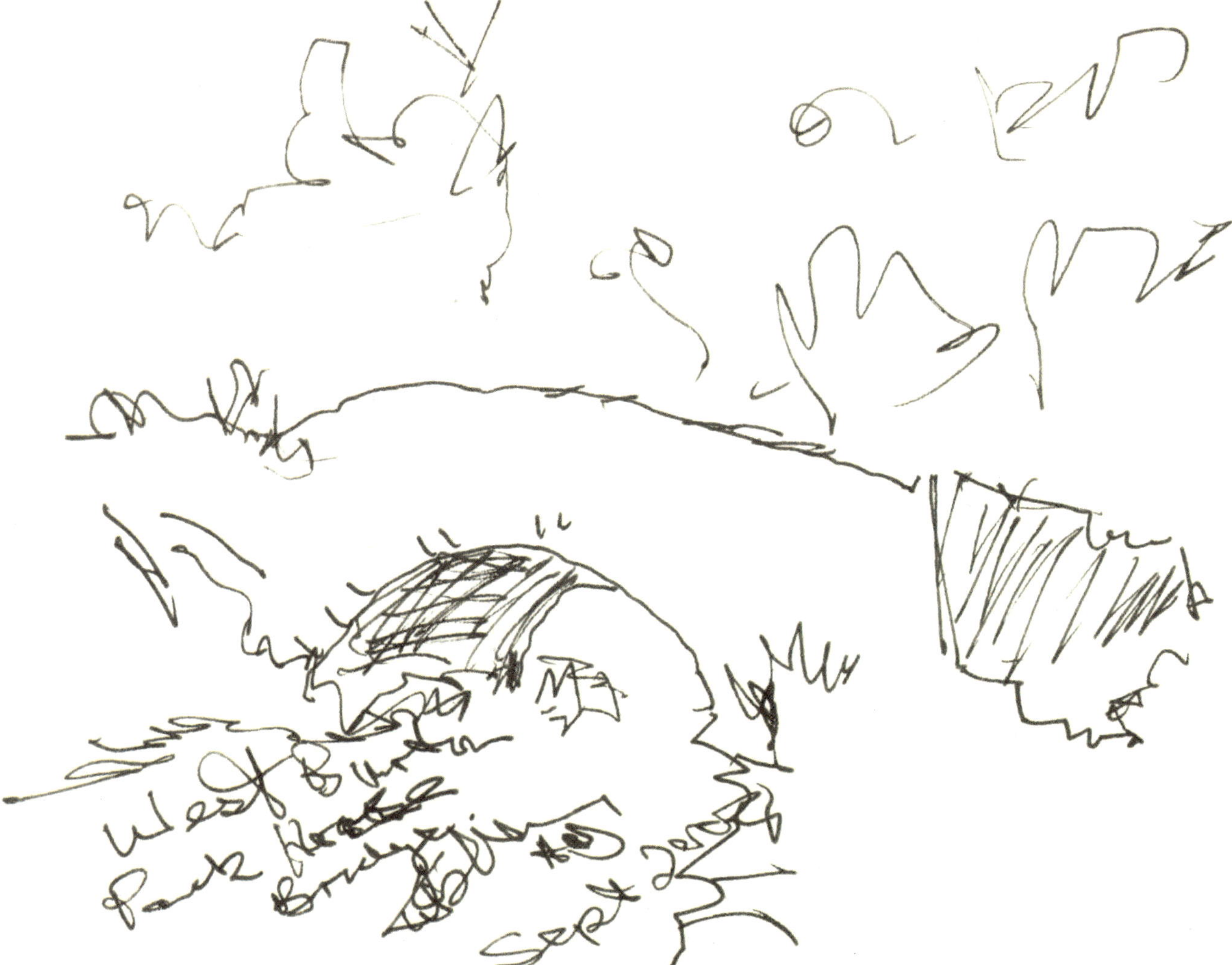

West Burton

I drew this in a quiet corner where the stream flows down from Kidstones Pass; it is the old packhorse bridge. It is a hidden gem away from the motorist; I hope not to spoil this by mentioning the location.

Gordale Scar (overleaf)

Its true size is only visible once you walk through the field alongside the beck and turn in to the scar itself.

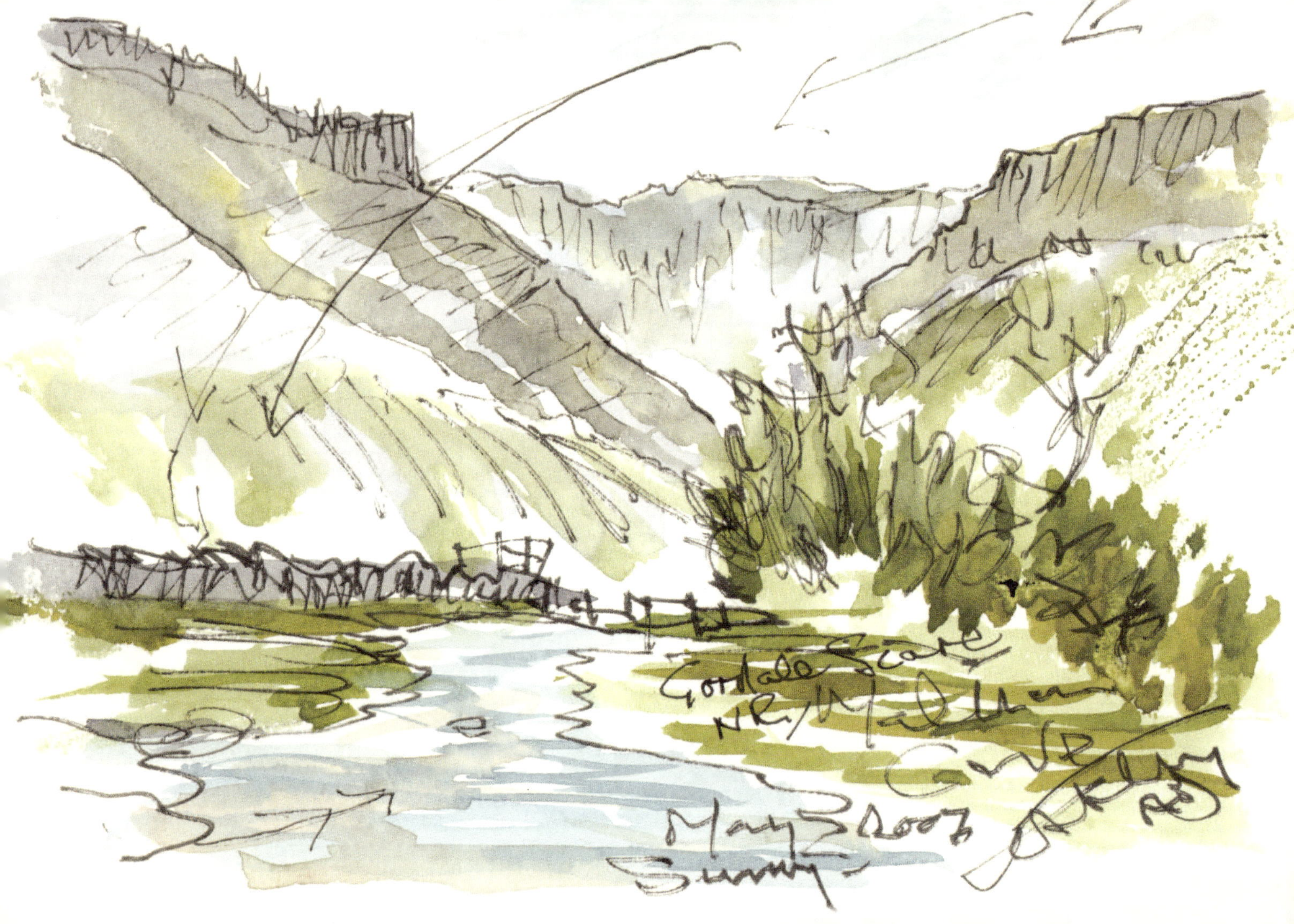
Gordale Scar
nr Malham
May 3 2007
Sunny

Malham

The view coming from Gordale Scar down to Malham village.

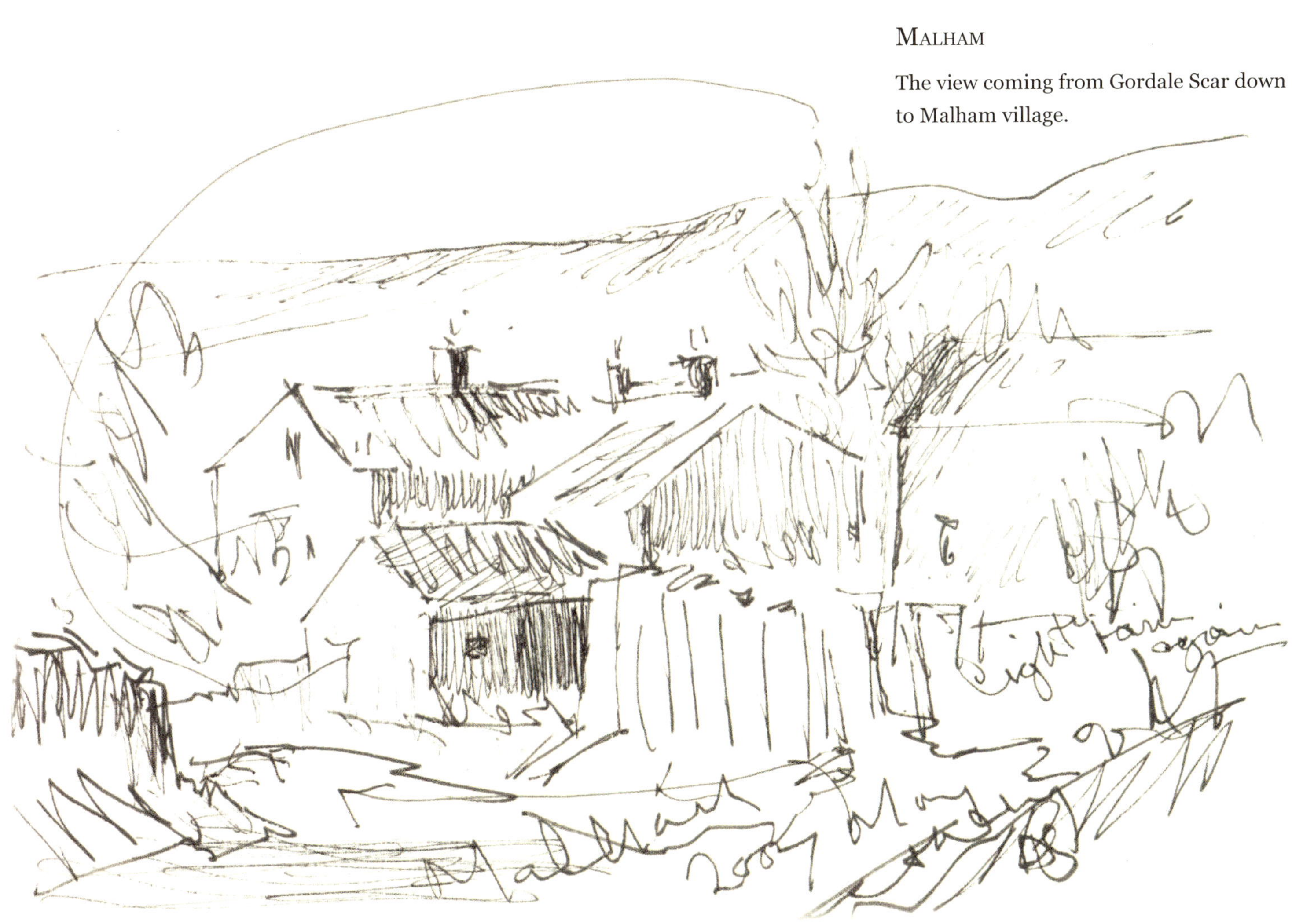

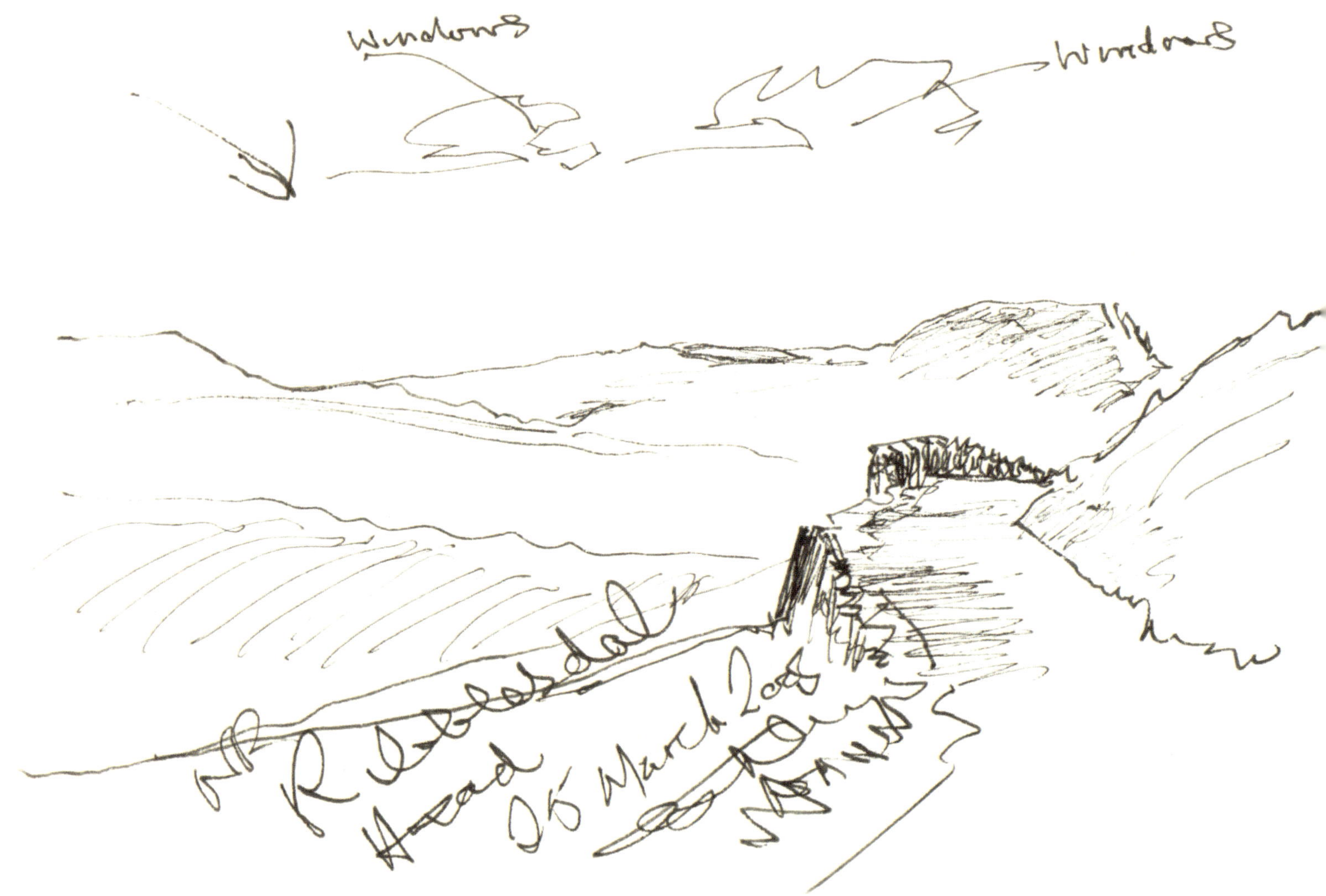
Windows
Windows

Ribblehead

A natural progression from the previous sketch. One of the western dales, whose river, the Ribble, drains in to the Irish Sea. Ribblehead is at the top of Ribblesdale and is itself famous for Ribblehead Viaduct, one of the must-see railway landmarks in England.

Ingleborough with farm in the mid-distance (overleaf)

Raining again and getting 'sodden' — a Yorkshire term for soaking wet.

Windows in the sky!

FARM

FARMS

25 March 2008 Rain again

Penyghent

Another fine Yorkshire day: it was raining, similar to the mist found out at sea.

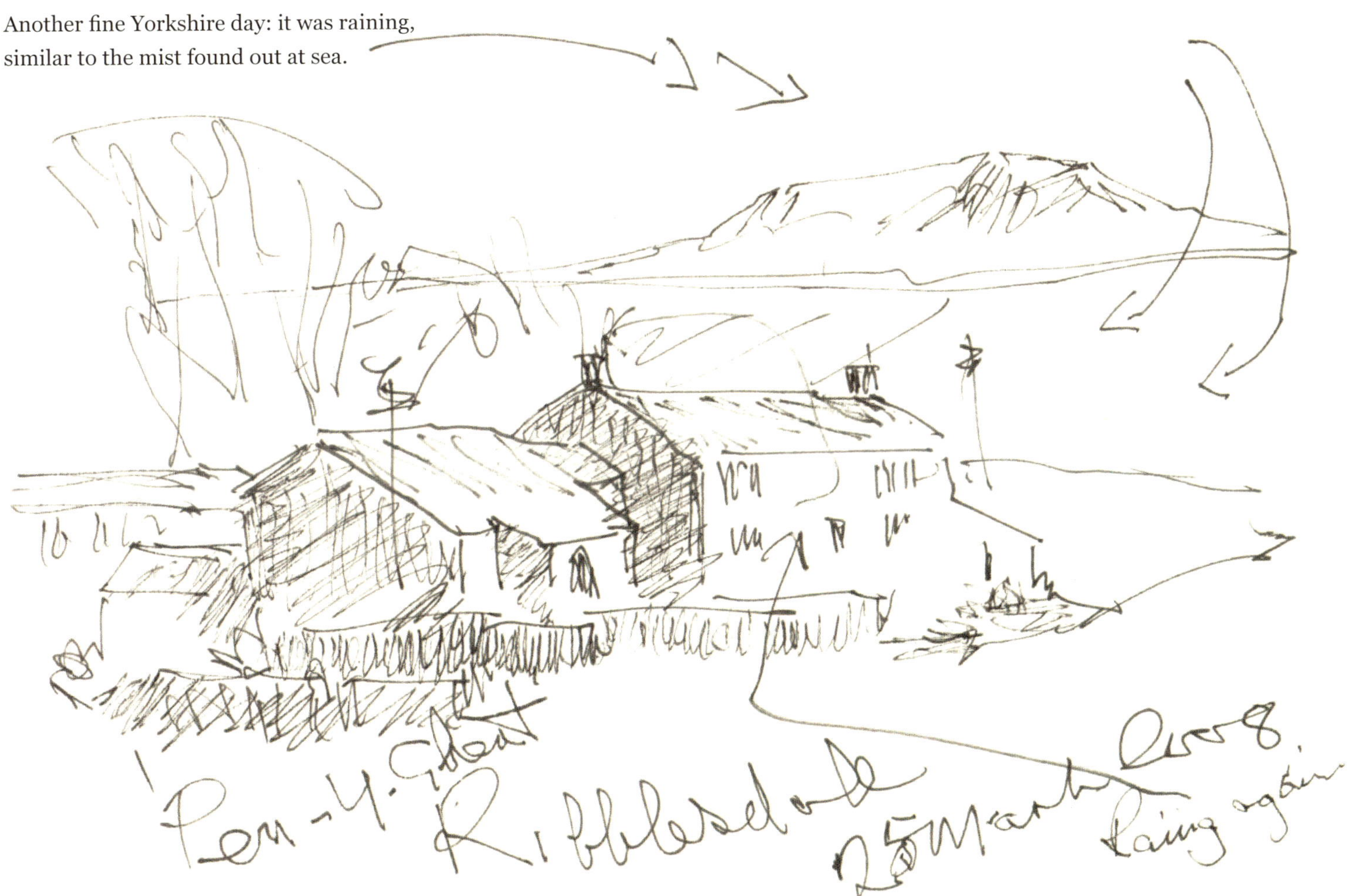

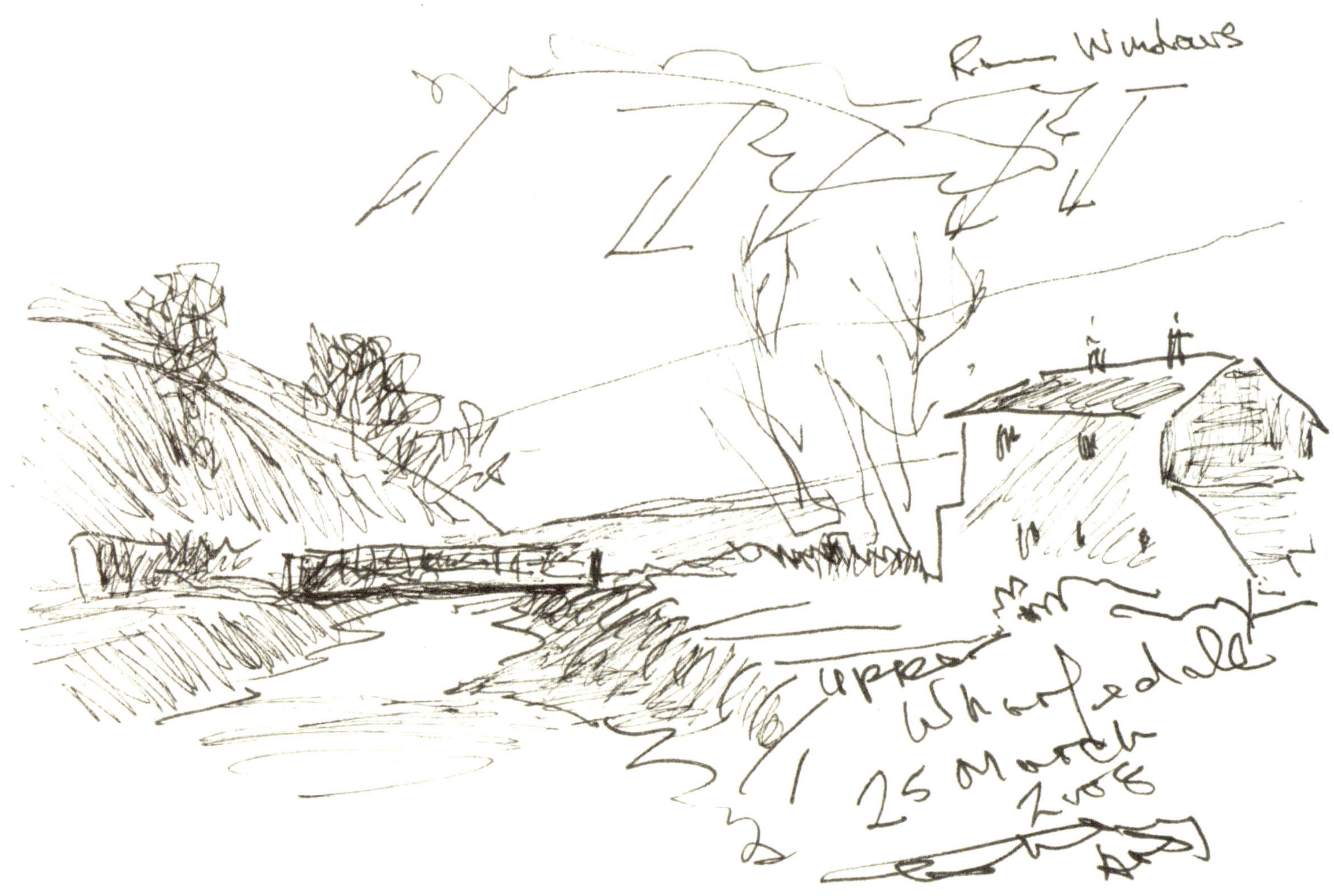
Upper
Wharfedale
25 March
2008

Upper Wharfedale

A classic U-shaped glacial valley. This is probably the most painted view in upper Wharfedale as it conveys the beautiful farming landscape. The road hugs the valley sides rather than running through the bottom of the valley due to the marshy ground limiting road-building opportunities. I have fond memories of this location as we filmed a series of *A Brush With Ashley* here with three students. Those were the days when YTV was at its best.

The George Inn, Hubberholme (overleaf)

I first discovered the George Inn in 1963 on my sketching tours in my little Mini van. I used to go in for a pint and sandwich, and was always amazed to find that the landlord was also the vicar of the church across the bridge, as it was one of the few pubs owned by the Church of England. This became a working sketch of an original painting that was later used for one of our Christmas cards.

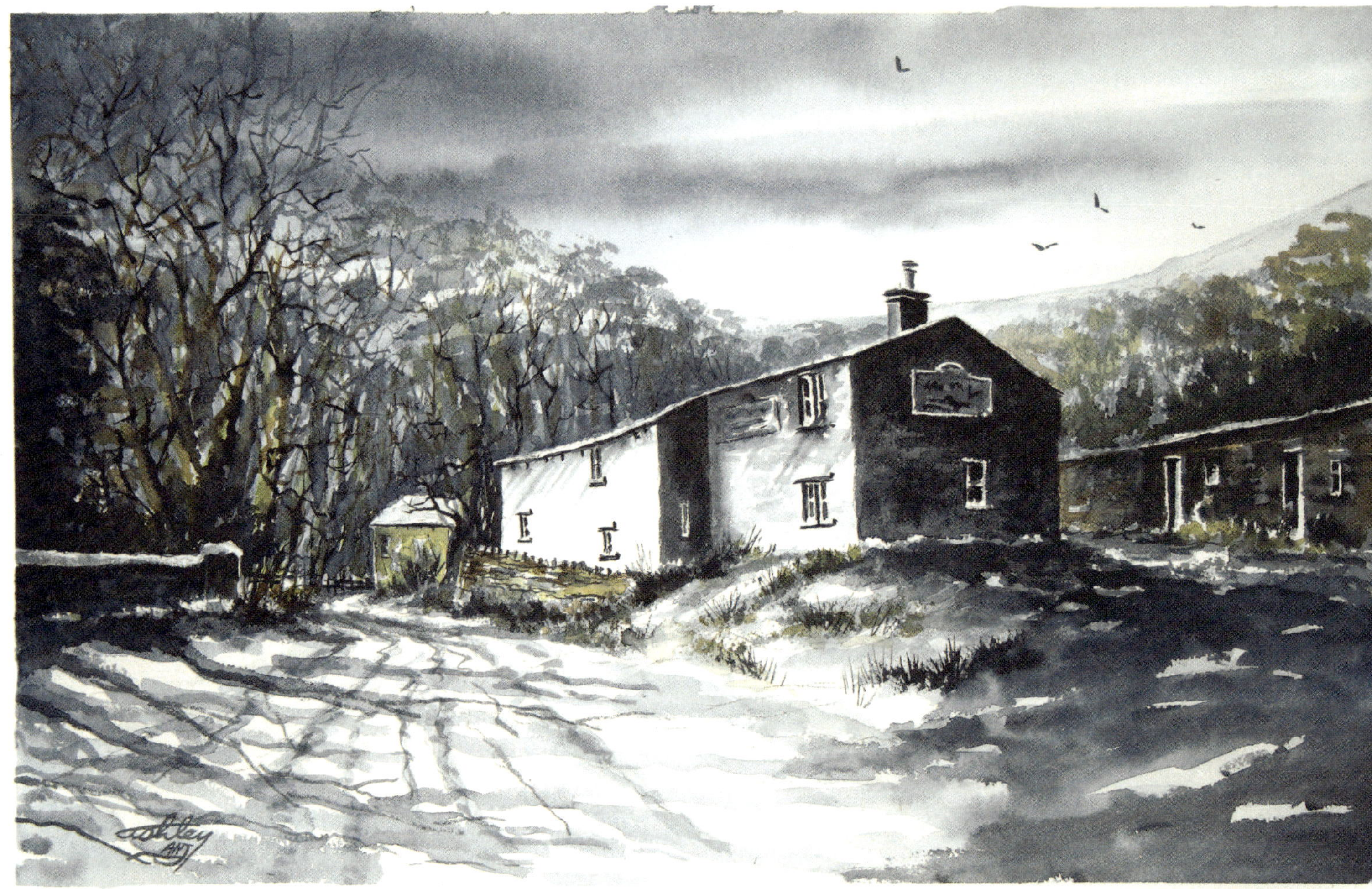

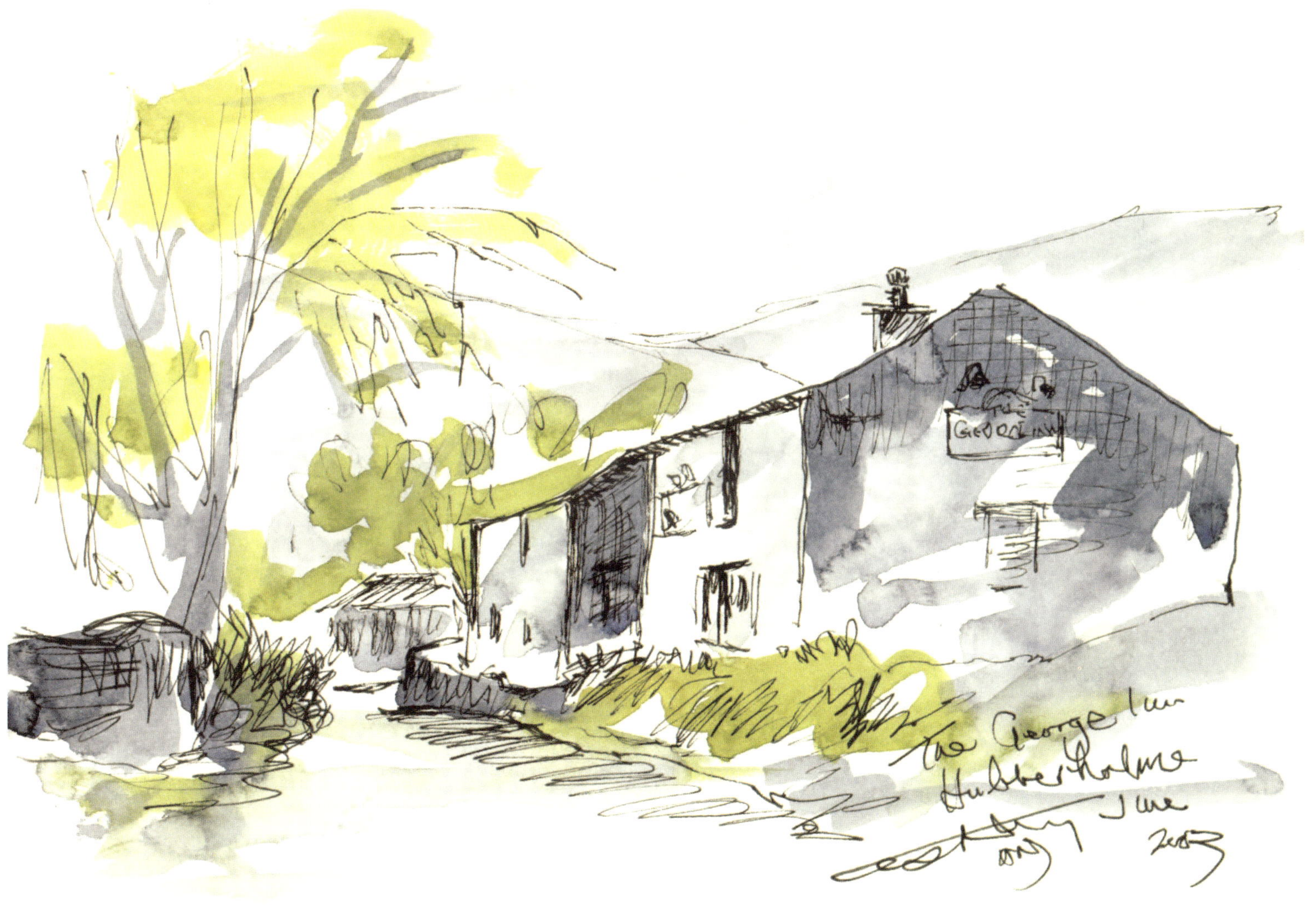
The George Inn
Hubberholme
June

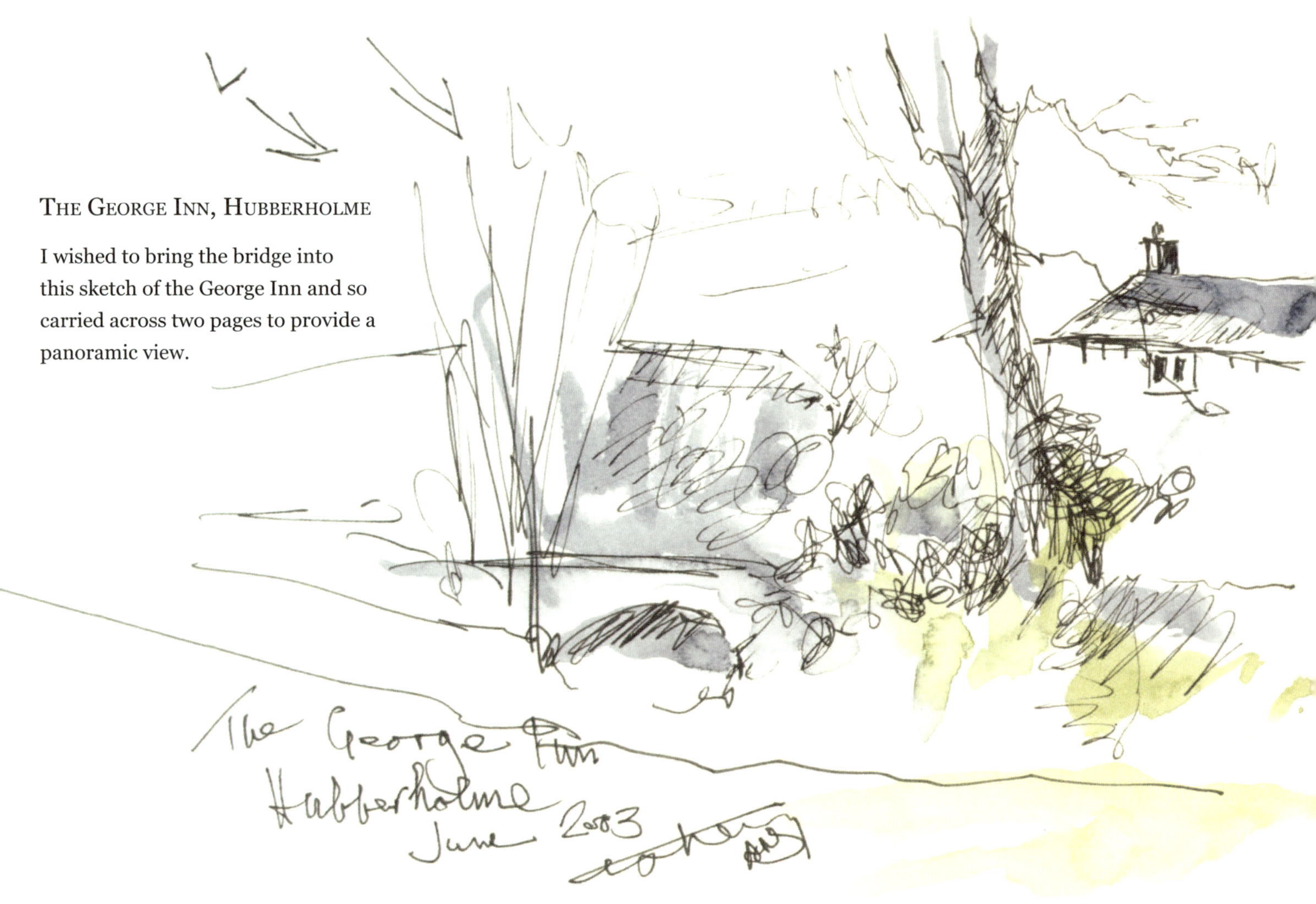

The George Inn, Hubberholme

I wished to bring the bridge into this sketch of the George Inn and so carried across two pages to provide a panoramic view.

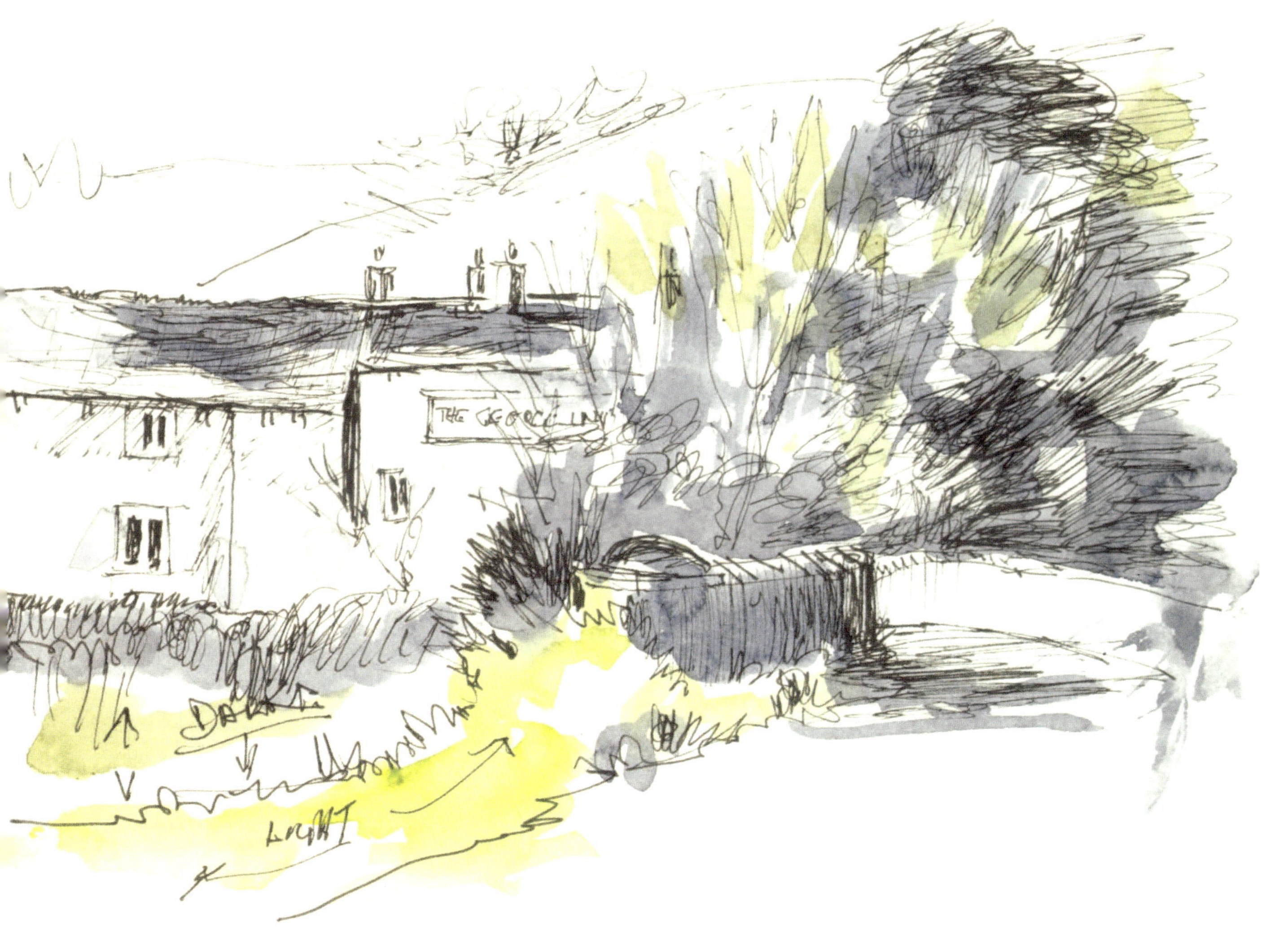
DARK
LIGHT

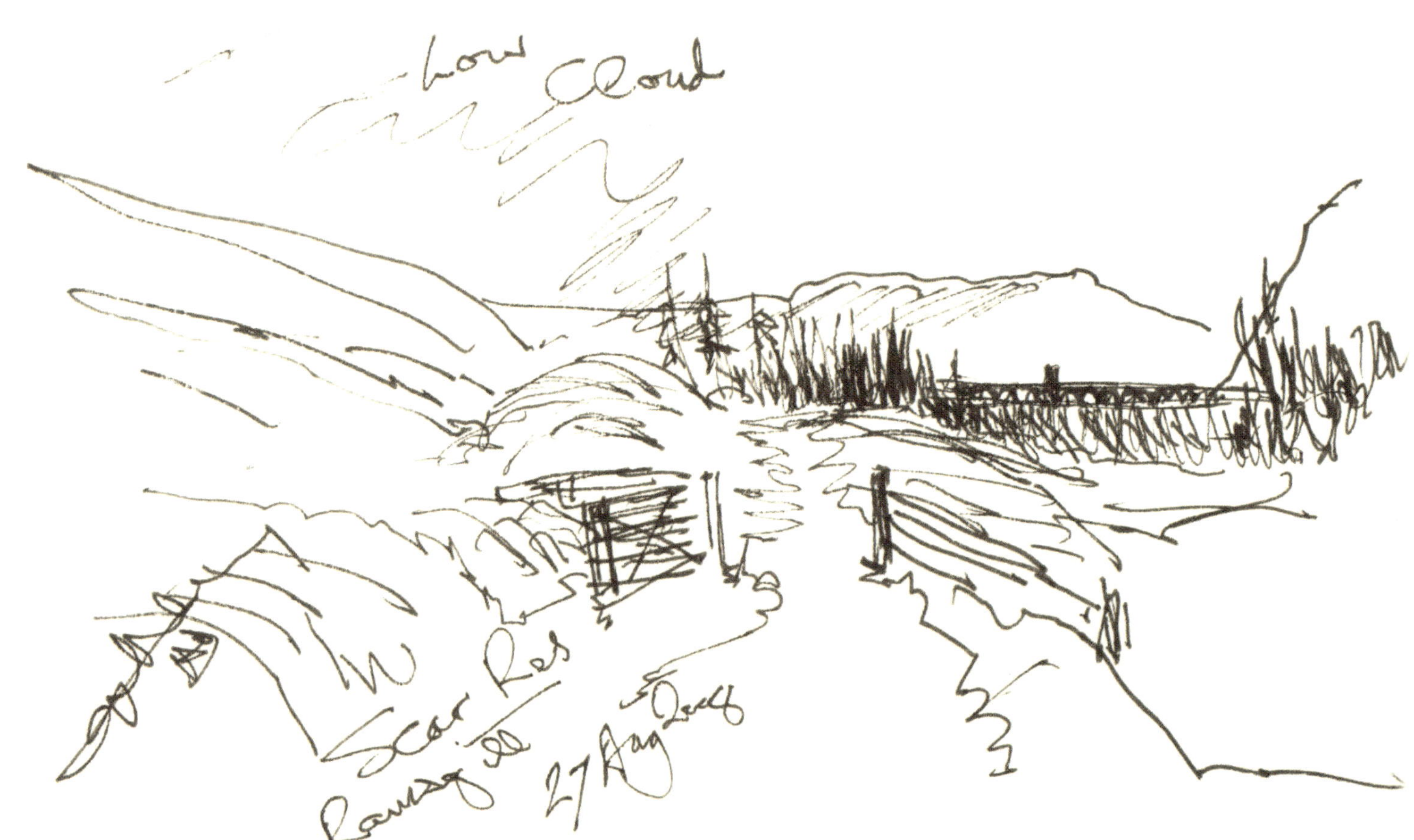
Low cloud
Scar Res
Ramsgill
27 Aug

Scar House Reservoir (left)

It is hard to believe, for it is long gone, that a whole village was created with a cinema and church for those constructing the reservoir. It reminds me of Tennyson's poem *All Things Will Die*. I love Tennyson's work as he was melancholic like me; at a party we would be called the two miserable sods.

Nidderdale (below)

This is an area of outstanding beauty, where the river Nidd flows the length of the valley.

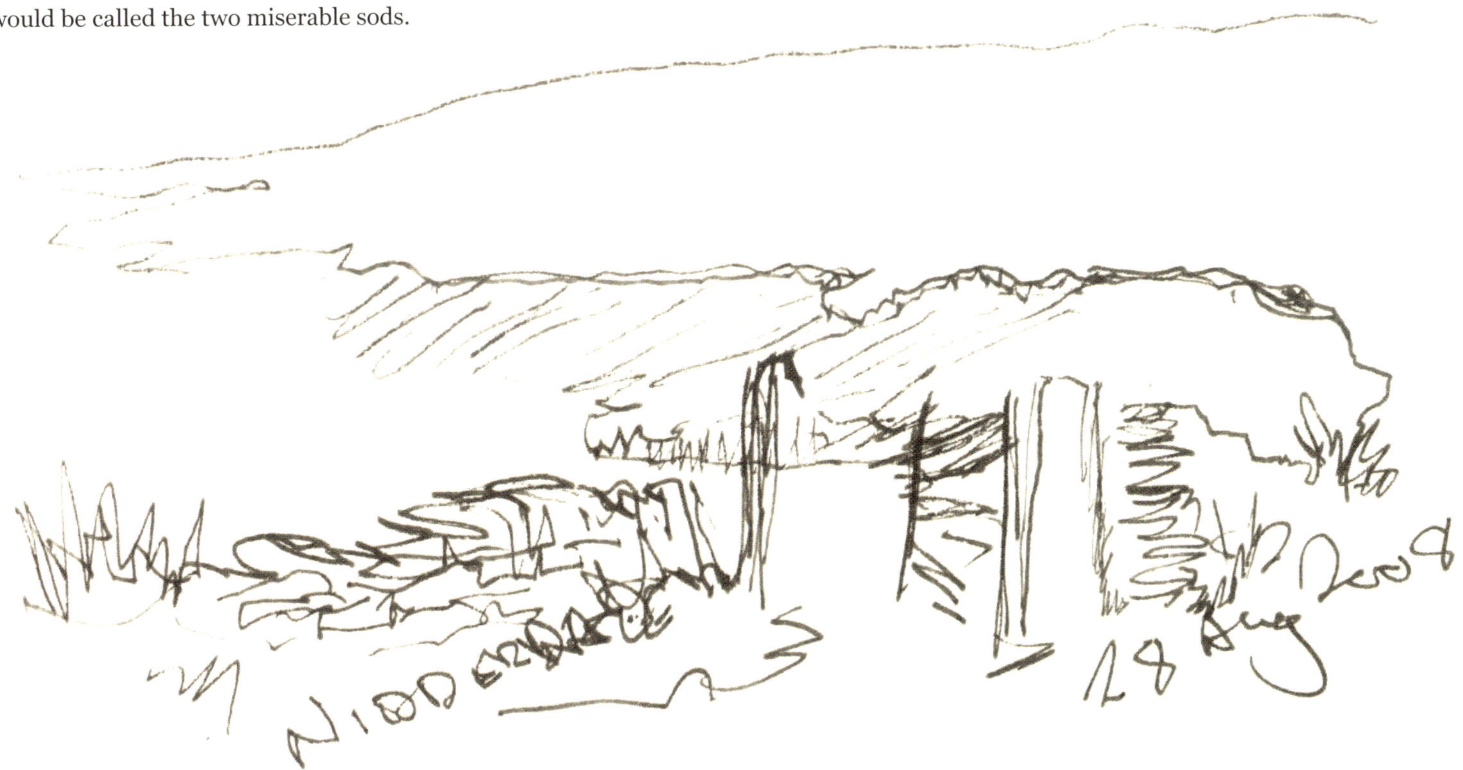

The sky is the drama of your painting,
you must see this drama
and hear the music of the land,
Feel the wind on your face
and smell the scent of the moor,
If you can smell it you can paint it

Ashley Jackson 1972

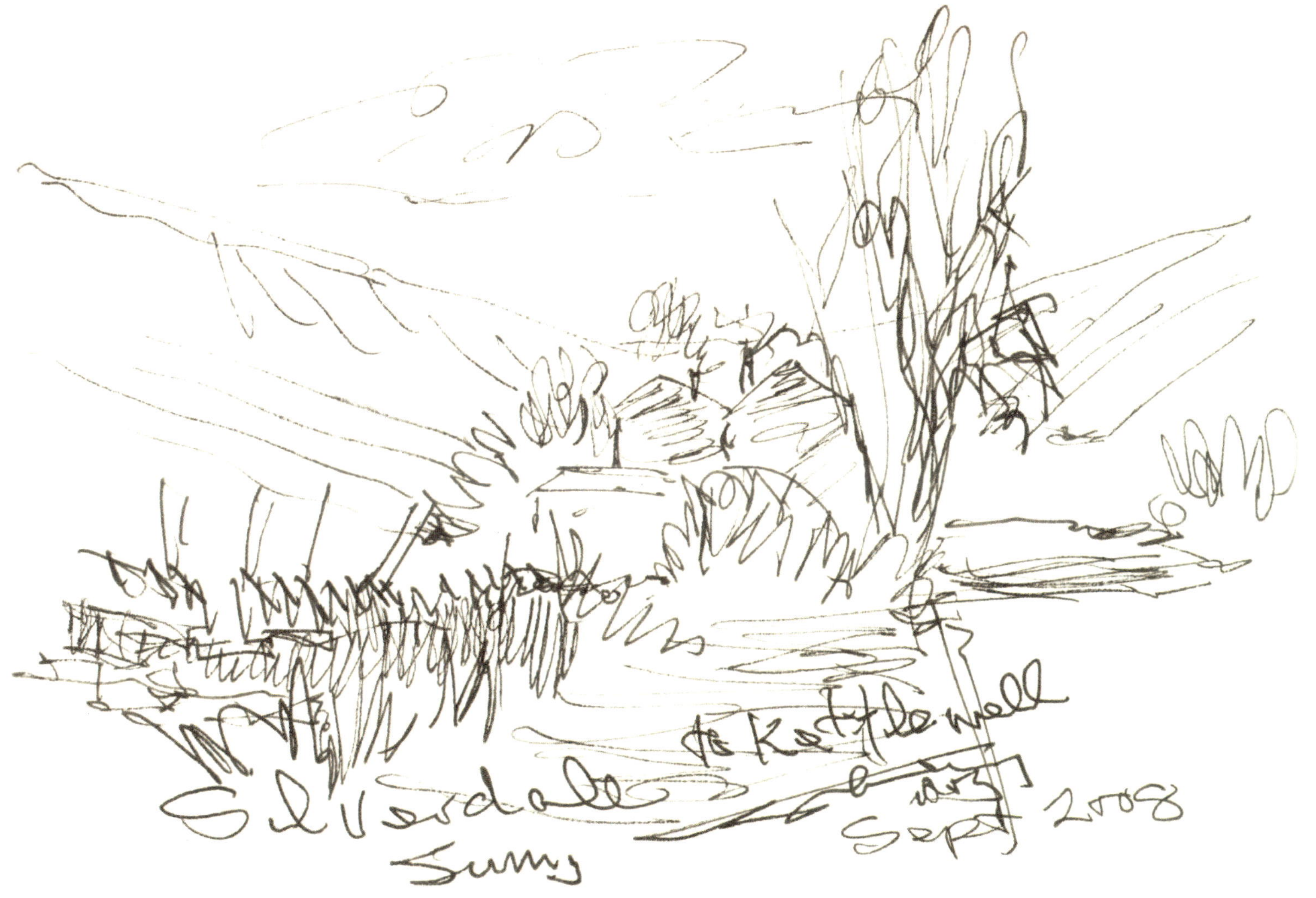
to Kettlewell
Silverdale
Sunny
Sept 2008

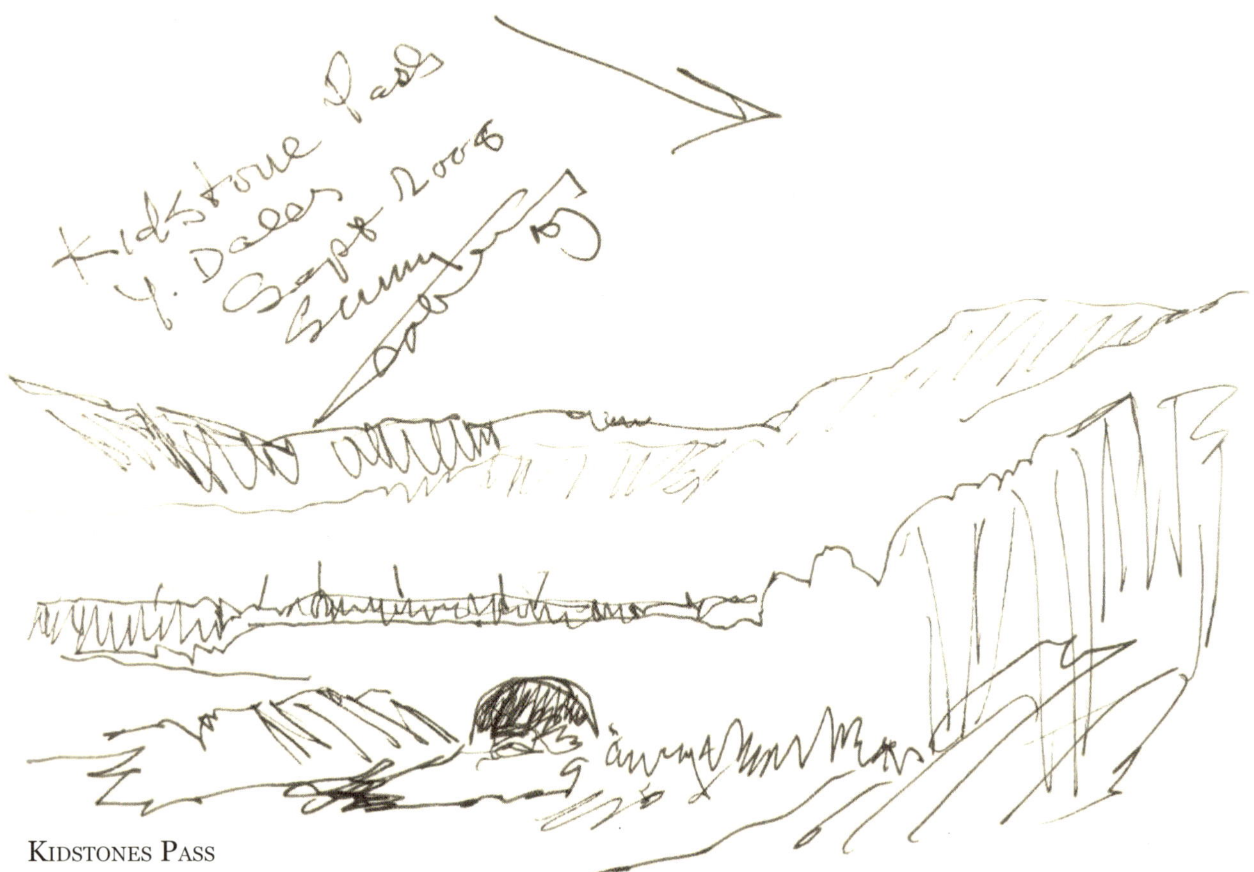

KIDSTONES PASS

I have always been criticised all my life ... Where is the sunshine in my paintings? Where are the bright colours? My answer is, when I was sixteen at art school, I wrote in my diary "I do not want to be the genius of the chocolate box", and "I want to do with the brush what the Brontës did with the pen". I want to create drama and atmosphere rather than pretty pictures. Nearby is the White Lion in upper Wharfedale, a member of CAMRA so you are assured of a good pint on your travels.

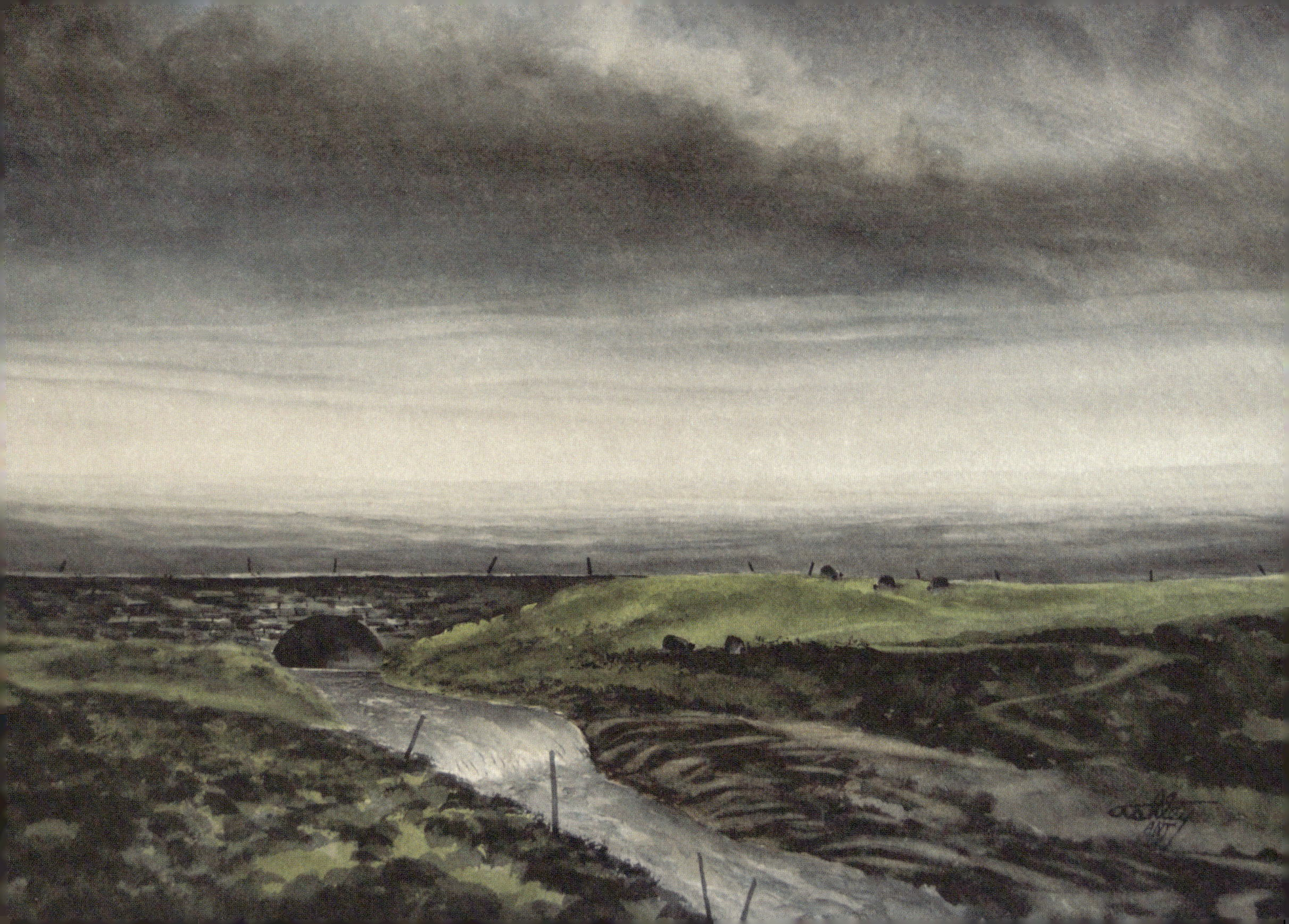

Slack Bottom

The title of the location always brings a smile to my face, as it reminds me of the day my old tutor at art school denoted the differences in the shapes of nudes for life drawing. He referred to Continental women having rounded bottoms. I spent the rest of the day walking around Barnsley looking at the differences in women's bottoms, for the sake of art of course! I could have been taken home by the police.

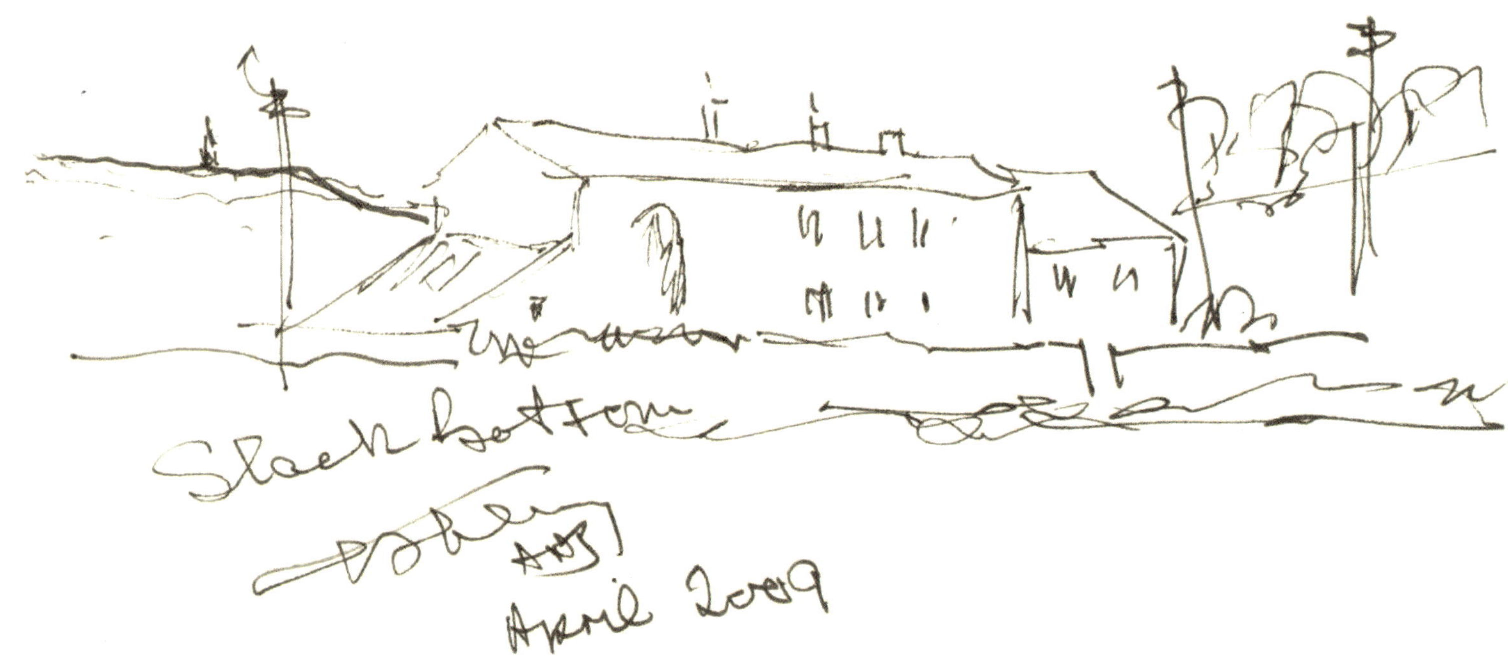

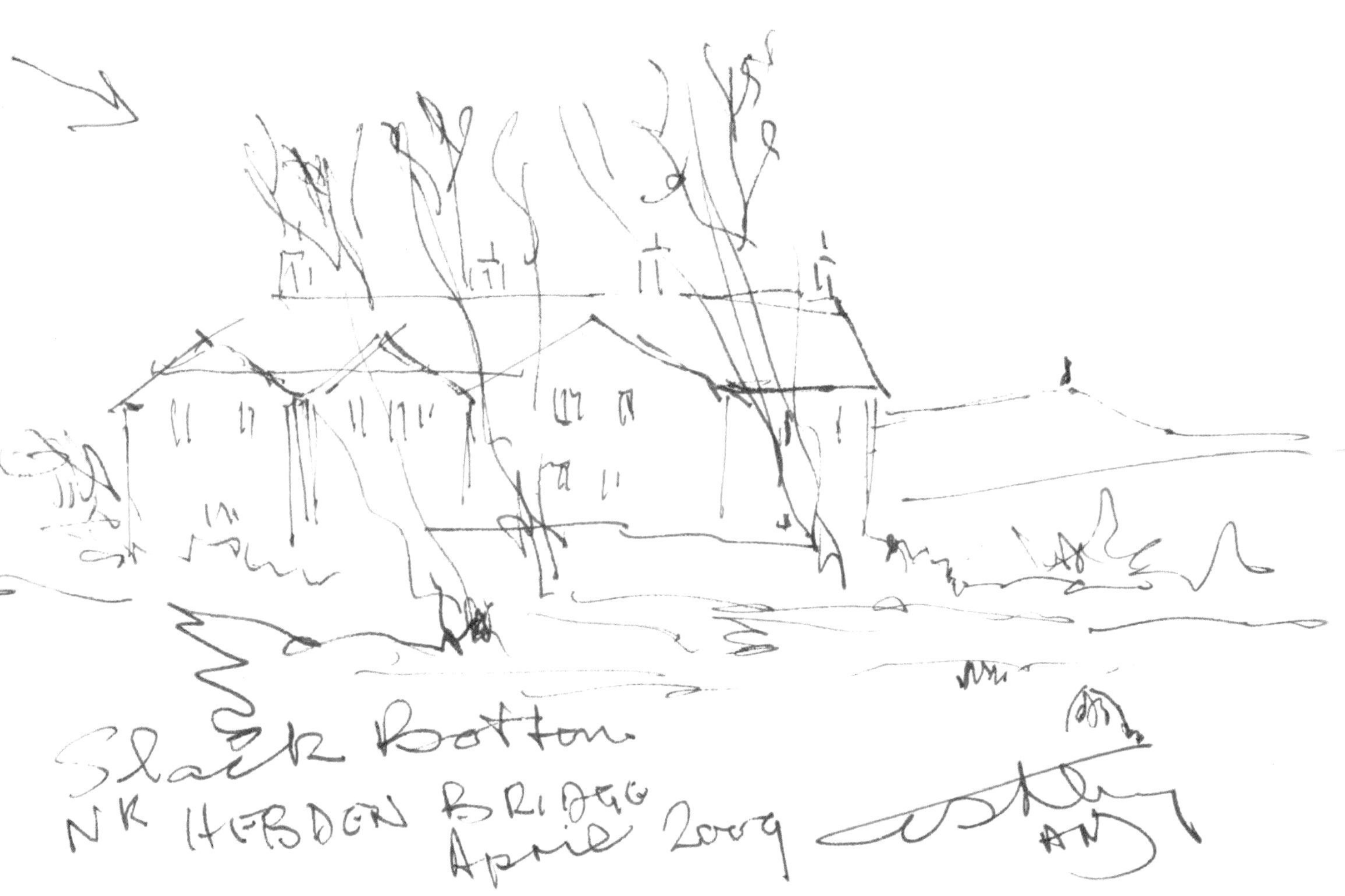
Slack Bottom
NR HEBDEN BRIDGE
April 2009

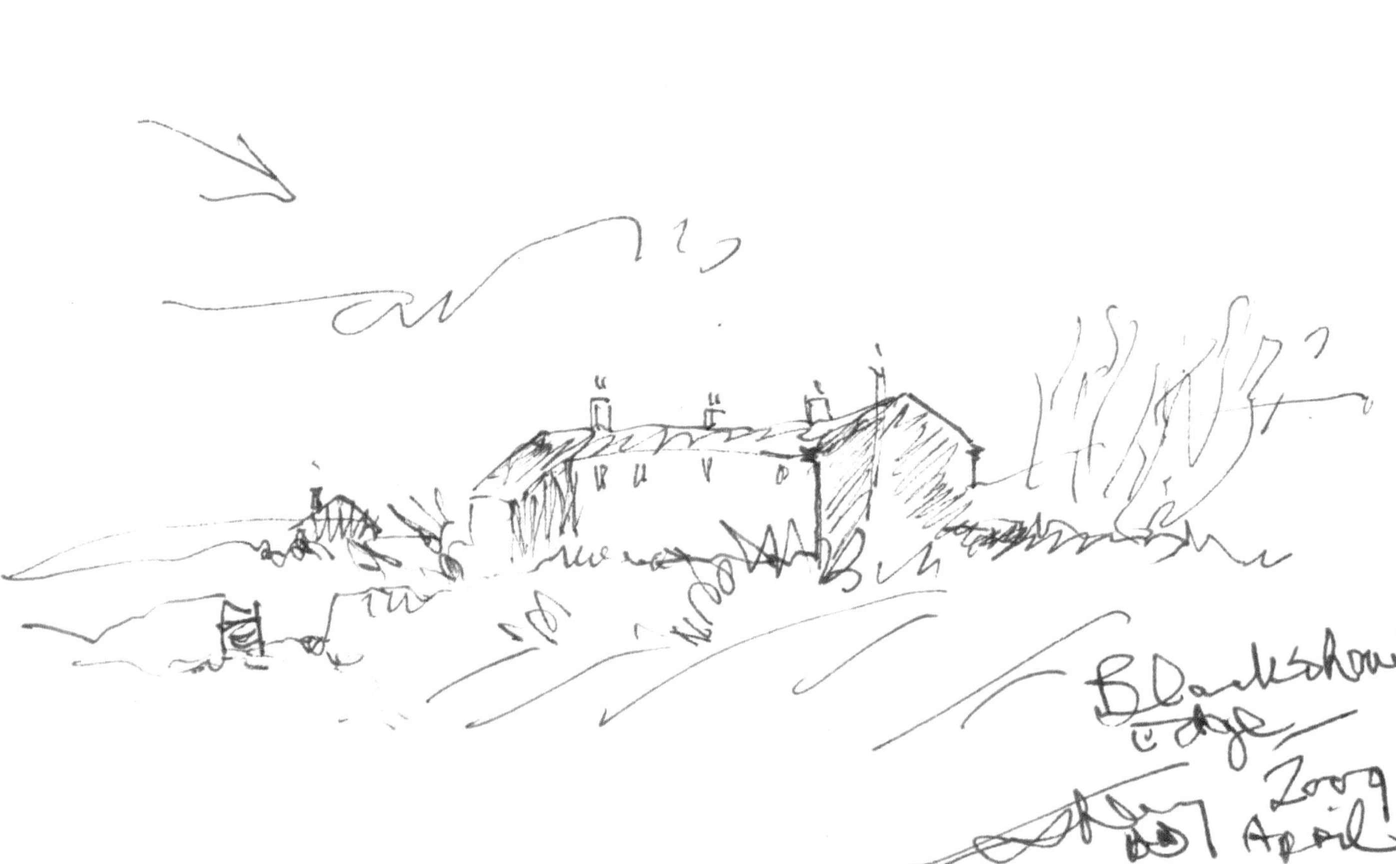
Blackshaw
2009
April

Blackshaw Edge with Stoodley Pike in the background

This location intrigues me. I don't believe in ghosts — or I thought I didn't. But whilst painting up here in the early 1970s I was approached by a little old lady who said that one day my work would be recognised and I would appear on television. She gave me a brown paper bag which contained half a dozen eggs. I was concentrating on my painting but asked her where she came from so that I could thank her later. She pointed to a farmyard and a caravan. Later I went down to the farm and asked the approaching farmer who the lady was. He replied that the caravan and the little old lady had been gone many years. To this day I still cannot work out how I had a brown bag of eggs in my hand ... Believe what you may.

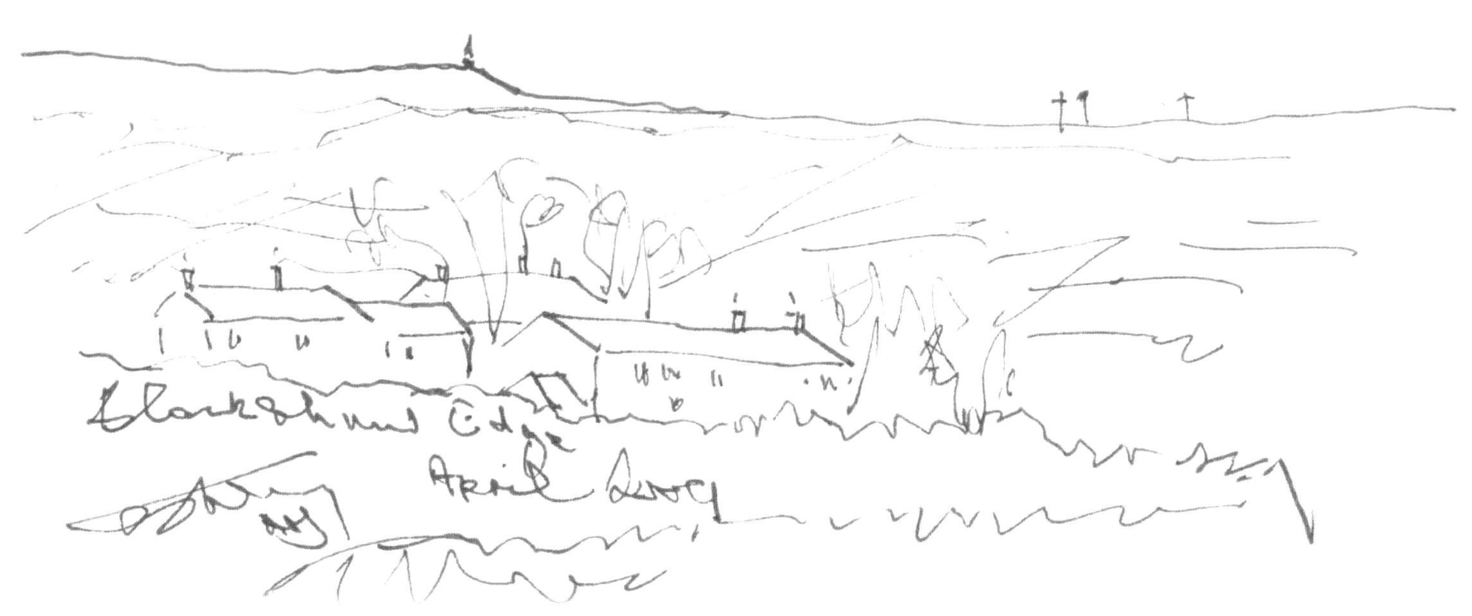

To see the spirit of Yorkshire and it's moors through your eyes is one thing;
Many people look but only a few will see and feel its very soul.

I wrote this in my sketchbook a number of years ago. With age I now liken this to a good glass of malt whisky: the colour and aroma are easy to recognise, but it is the hidden depth of the taste of peat and its recognition in the senses that does not reveal itself to all. Yorkshire is the same; it is there for all who want to enjoy it but, being selfish, I am glad that not everyone can appreciate it as my vocation would be much more difficult if the landscape was full of people.

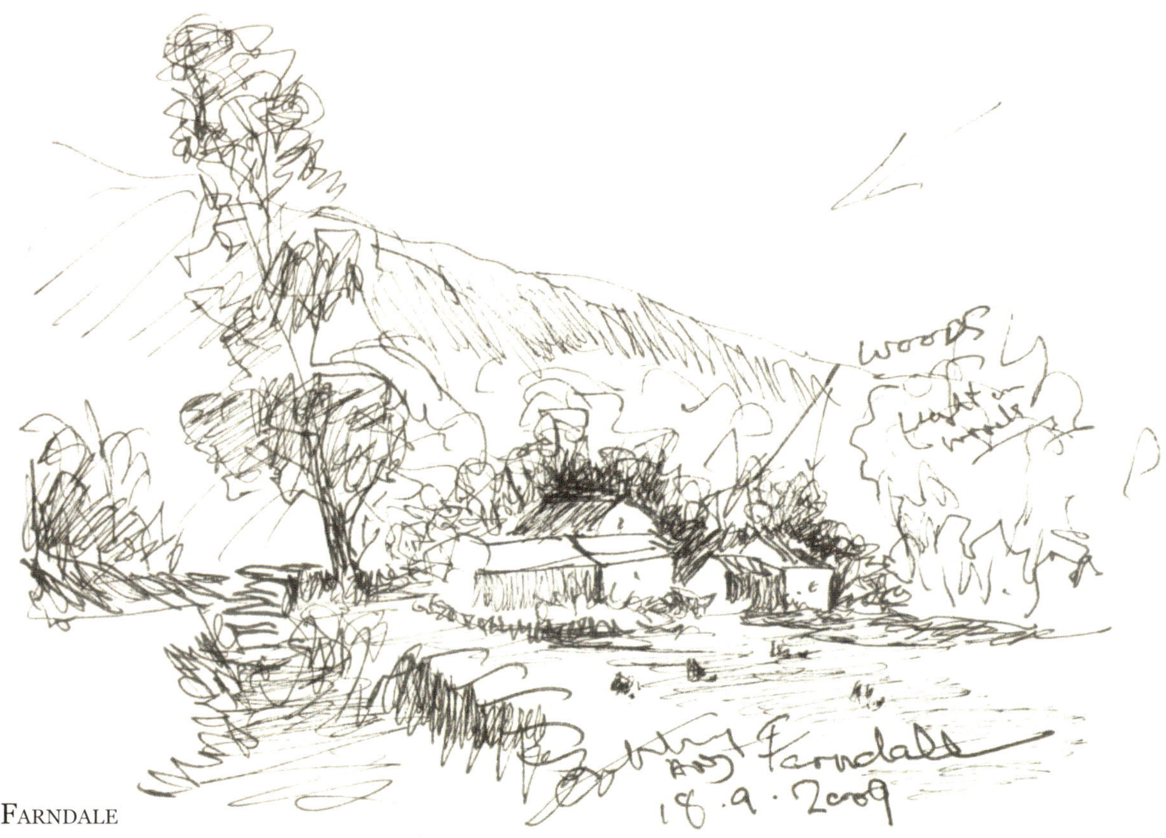

FARNDALE

This was a challenging day — one when I could so easily have packed up and gone home. Mother Nature does this at times when she wants to shut you out to keep the experience to herself. One has to be a romantic about the situation, where not only the scene comes in to play but the feeling, what is she trying to tell you. I have always said that if you cannot feel it, you won't be able to paint it. Unfortunately 'it' isn't quantifiable or even tangible; it is the intimate relationship you share with the painting. Like Dorian Gray, it is your soul and raw emotion. You cannot squeeze it out of a paint tube it has to be felt.

West Nab

The farm on the hilltop rises to the challenge of all the elements thrown at it by Mother Nature. It is a solid farm, built like the hardy folk that live within it, tending to the land and the animals to make a way of life.

Winscarr above the Holme Valley

This reservoir nestles in the moors surrounding Holmfirth and Langsett. It is a place I used to frequent long before I had a car and I used to take the bus to transport me to my painting locations. When you are catching a bus to go sketching, you go what ever the weather, as more often than not you have booked the day off to go; but today if you have a car you choose to go out only on nice days. A true lover of the countryside is out in all weathers, seeing Yorkshire in all her moods. We just go prepared for rain, snow and sunshine — for Yorkshire is the only county that can have all seasons in one day.

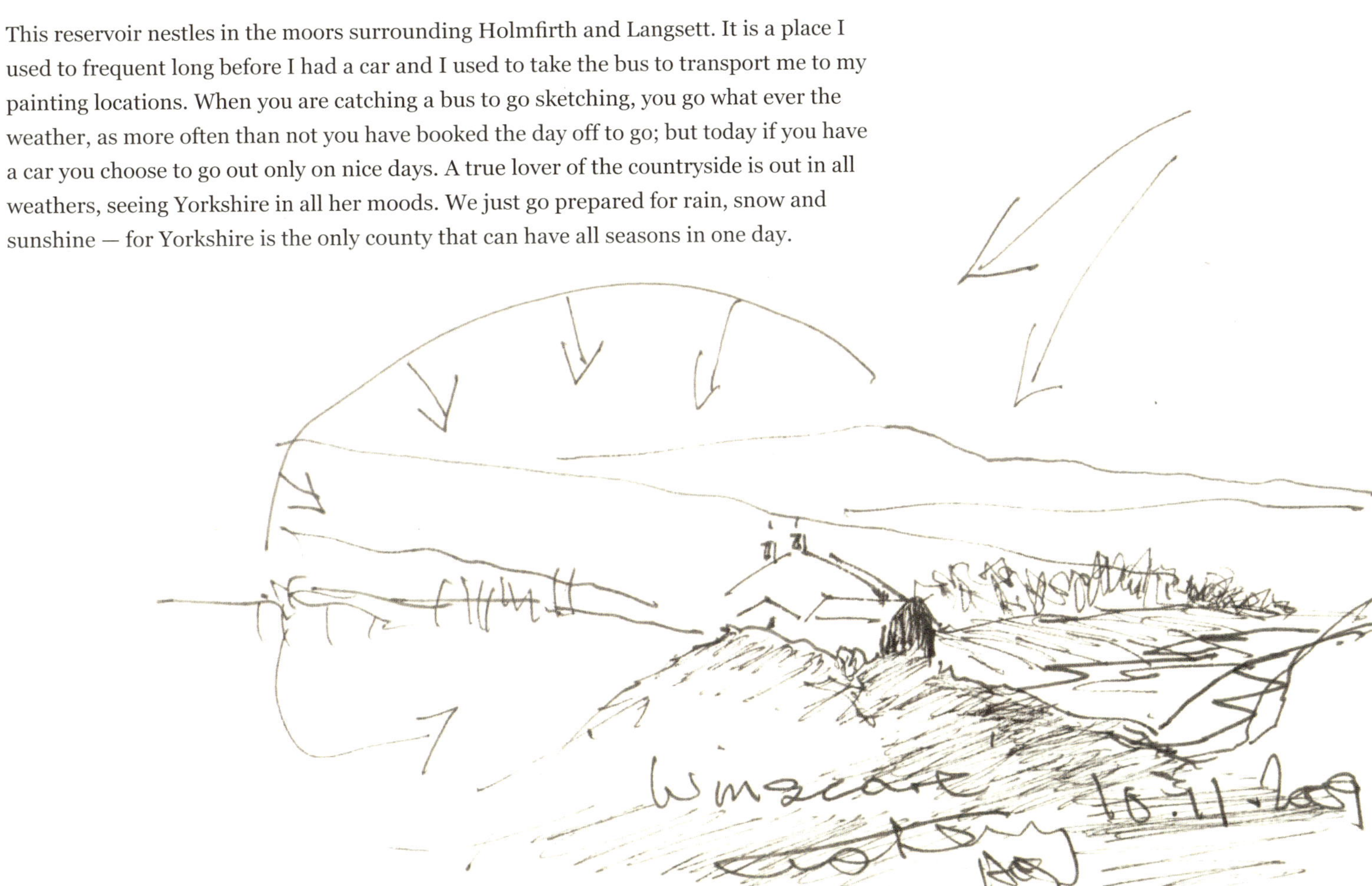

White House on Haworth Moor

This was included in one of my programmes *A Brush With Ashley*. It is just a couple of miles outside Haworth, with the moors surrounding it and Top Withens (Wuthering Heights) in the far distance. Withens is a Yorkshire term meaning 'wild'.

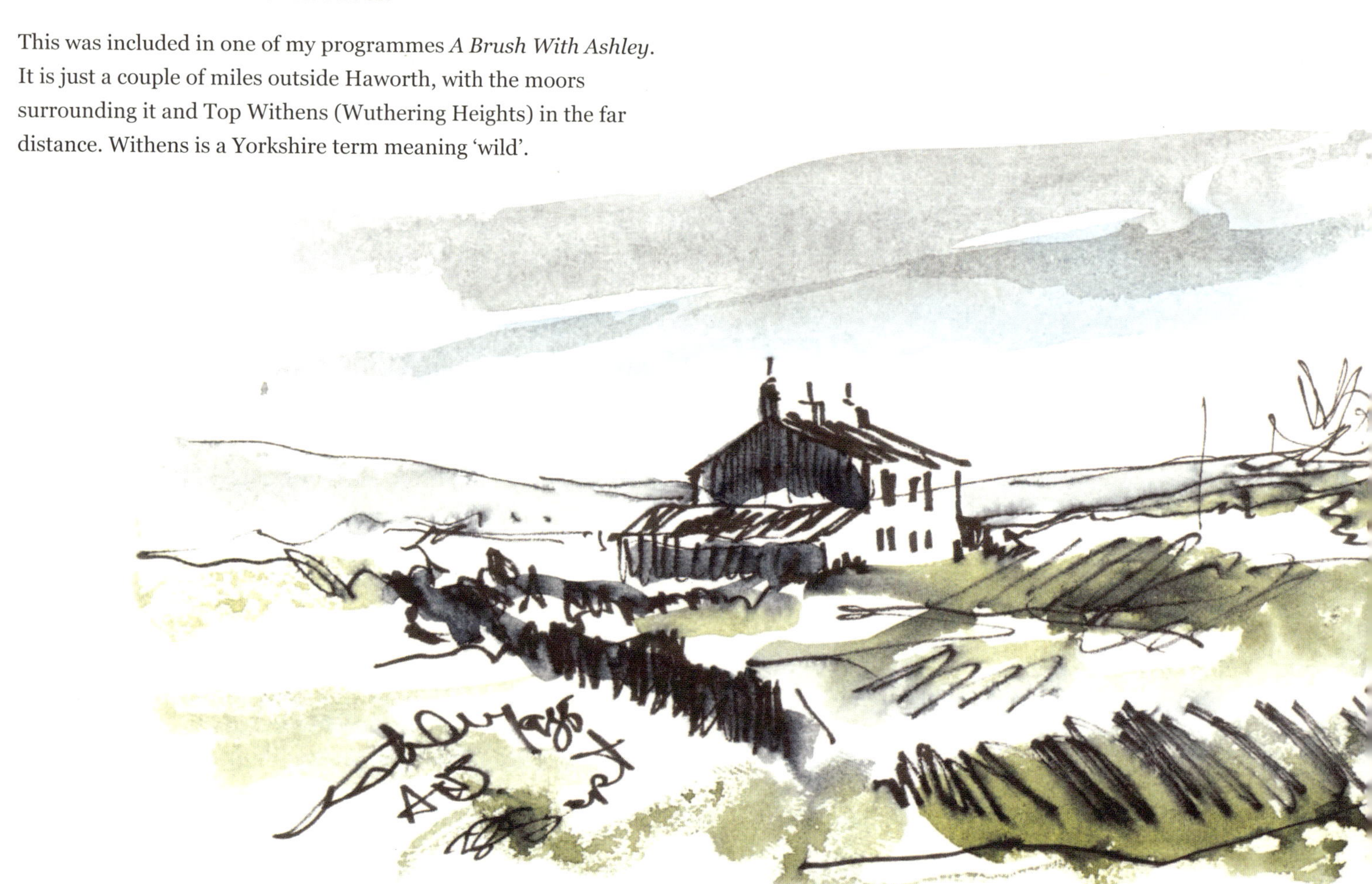

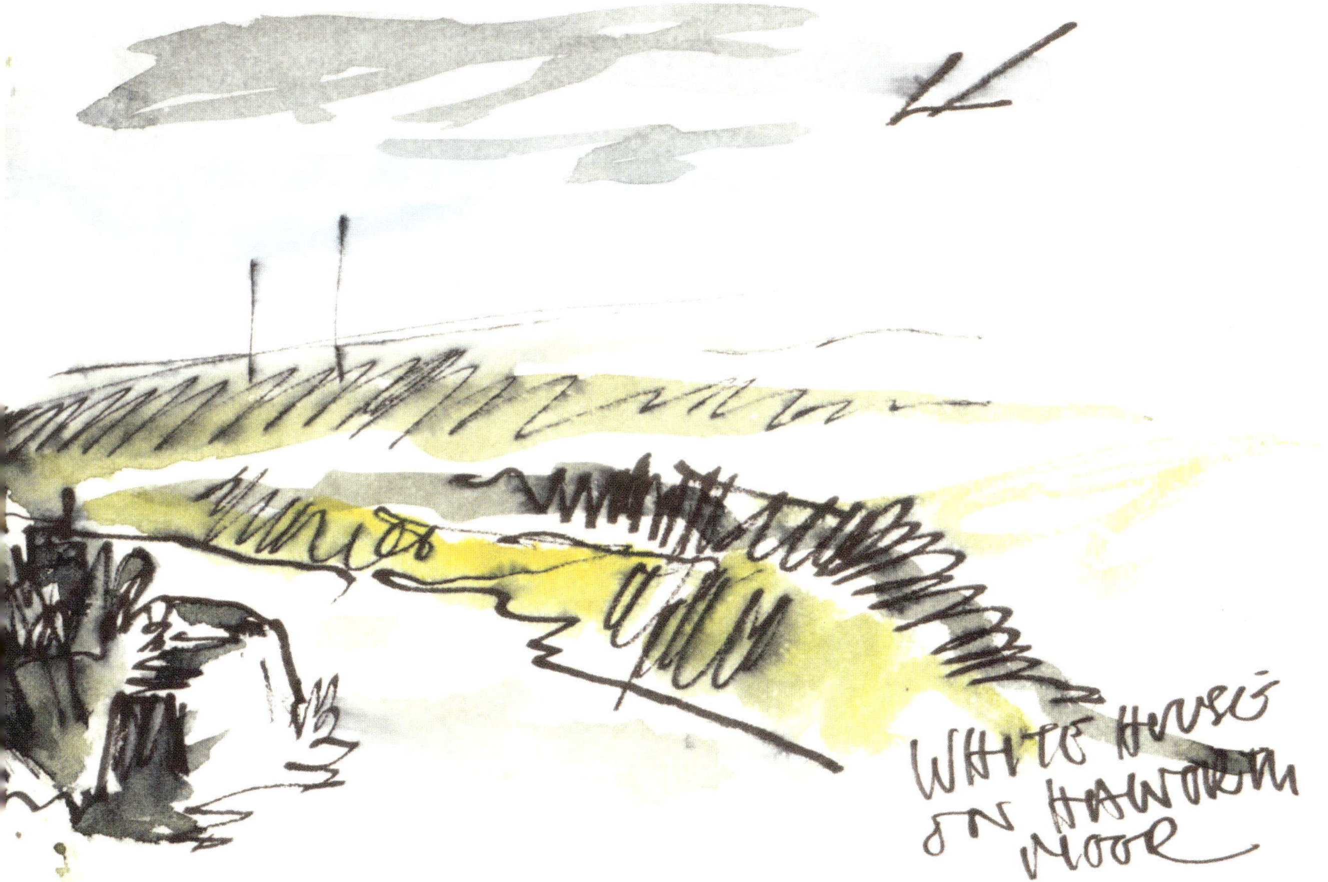

WHITE HOUSE
ON HAWORTH
MOOR

Fremington Edge

The light on this day was bouncing off the moorland fells and lighting up the farm.

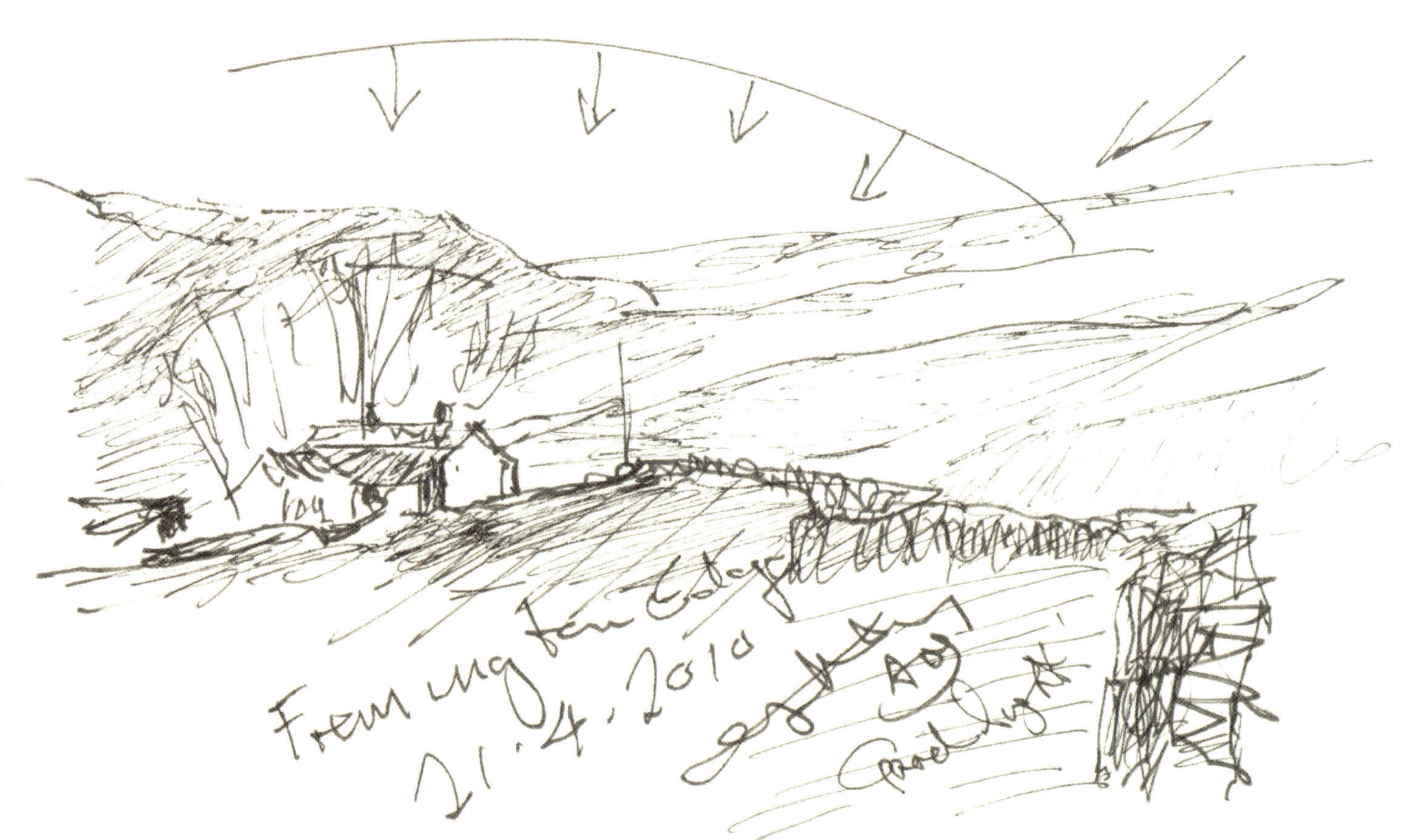

Calva View

This is an enchanting little corner of upper Swaledale going on to Tan Hill; it is a jewel of a location.

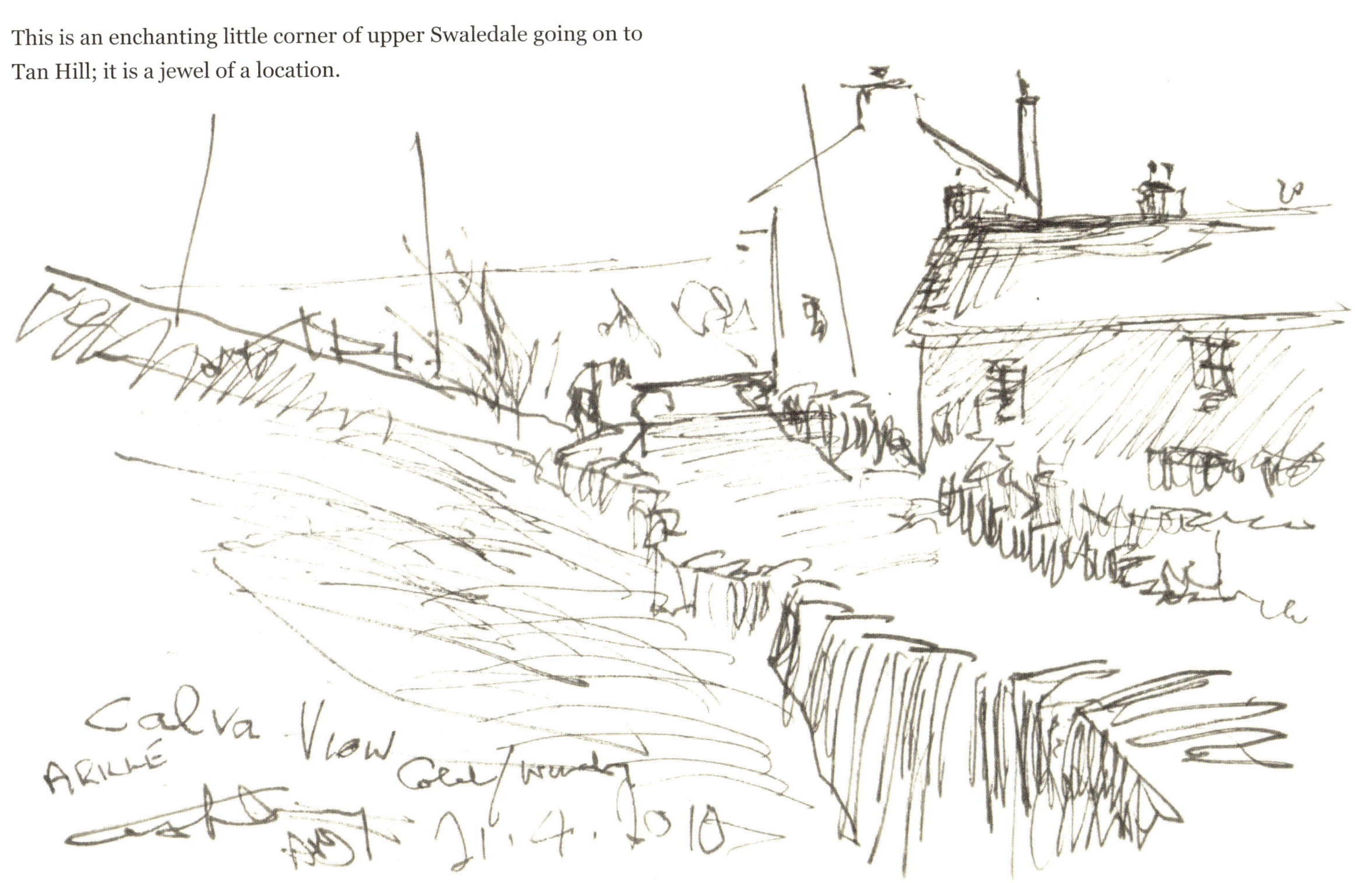

Middleham Castle

I first discovered Middleham Castle coming in through the back door so to speak, from the Leeds-Harrogate side rather than the A1M turning in to Bedale and seeing Middleham from the other side of the valley.

This was drawn from where Turner, the greatest English landscape artist, once stood and painted. He toured Yorkshire and its dales on horseback.

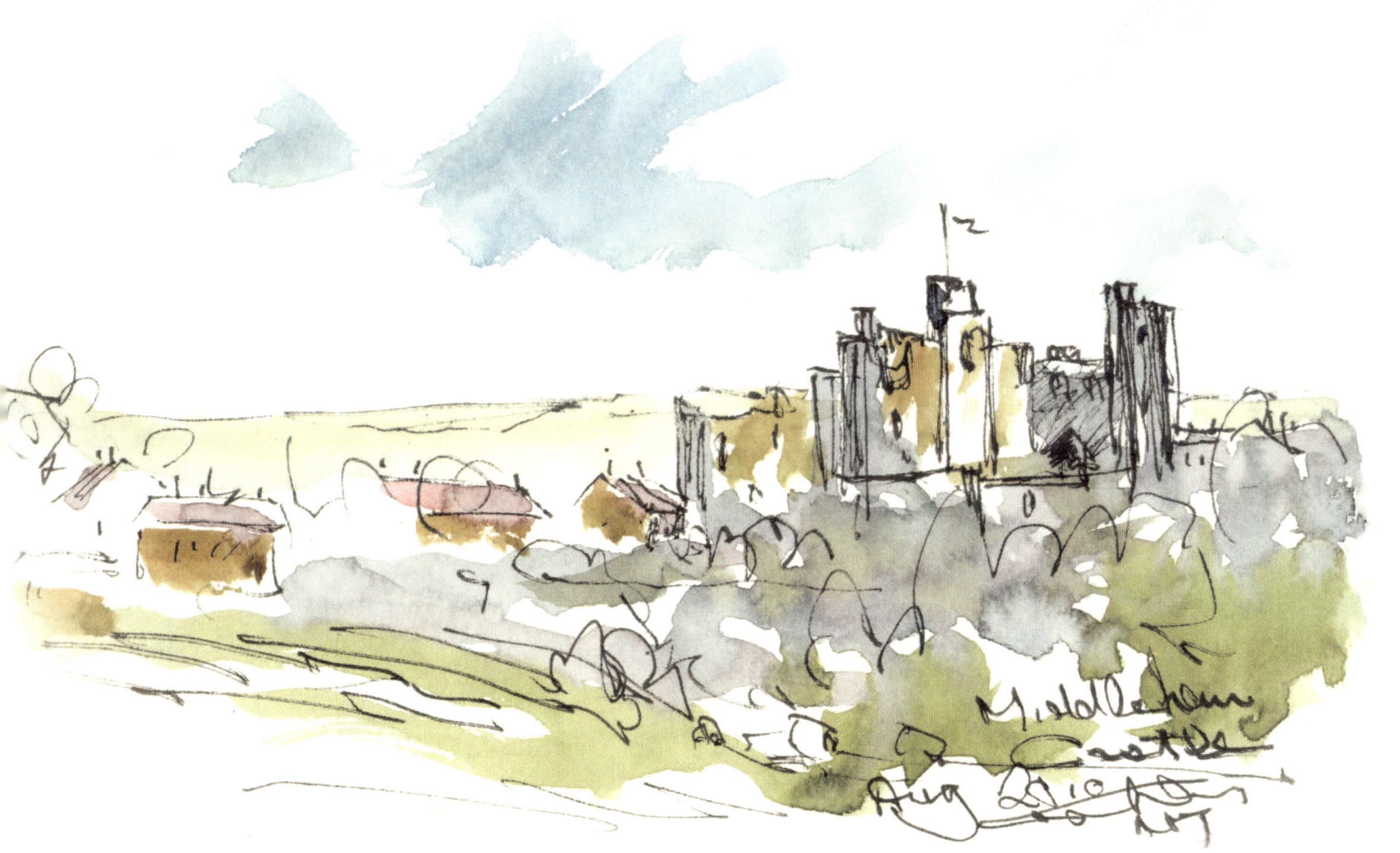

Tan Hill Inn (below)

Rumour has it that a previous landlady was buried behind the inn in an outcrop of rocks, such was her desire not to leave her beloved landscape. The inn is a monument to human beings and their ability to survive in hostile climates living away from humanity. It sits upon the frozen seas of the landscape like a ship on the ocean. There can be no good or bad weather days up here – they are all 'surviving days'.

Hardraw (right)

A lovely quaint hamlet with the Green Dragon pub and a small village church close together. To see Hardraw Force you have to go through the pub and make your way up to the Force, a long single line of water cascading over a hundred feet. In my youth I climbed up the Force to the waiting moorland at the top, not something I would recommend today. My wife and I for many years had a static caravan at Mrs Hessledean's where the address was Henry's, the Green, Hawes. We had many a happy time there with our two daughters, sketching and walking.

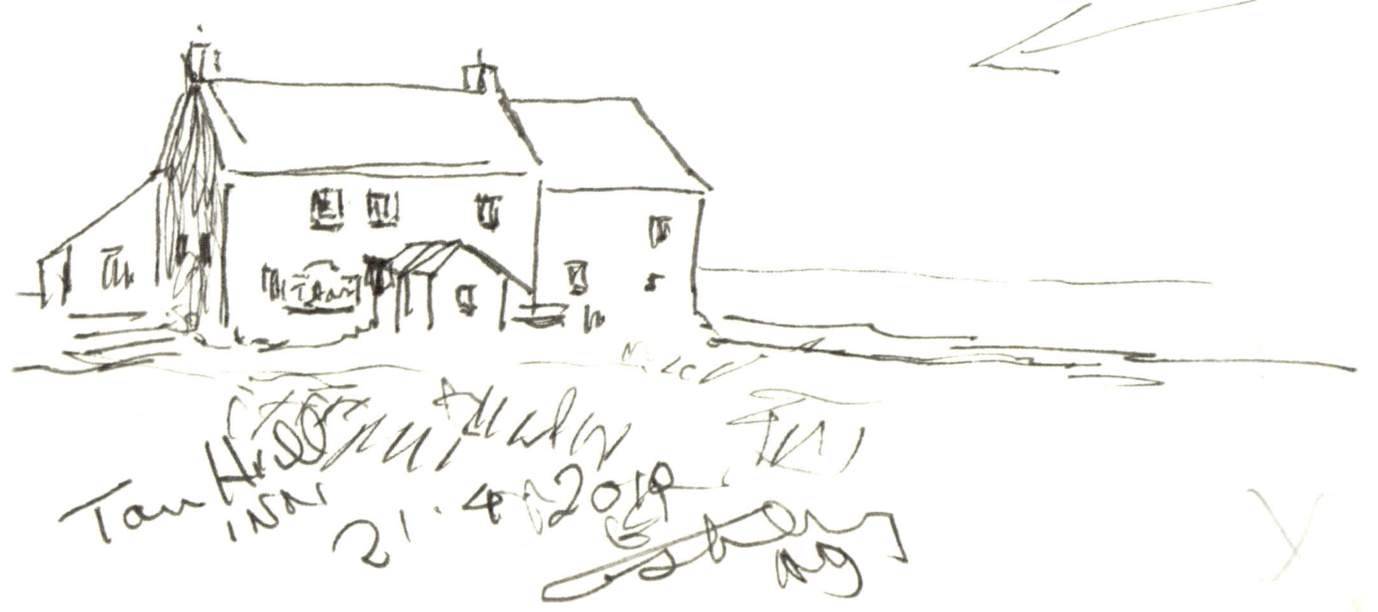

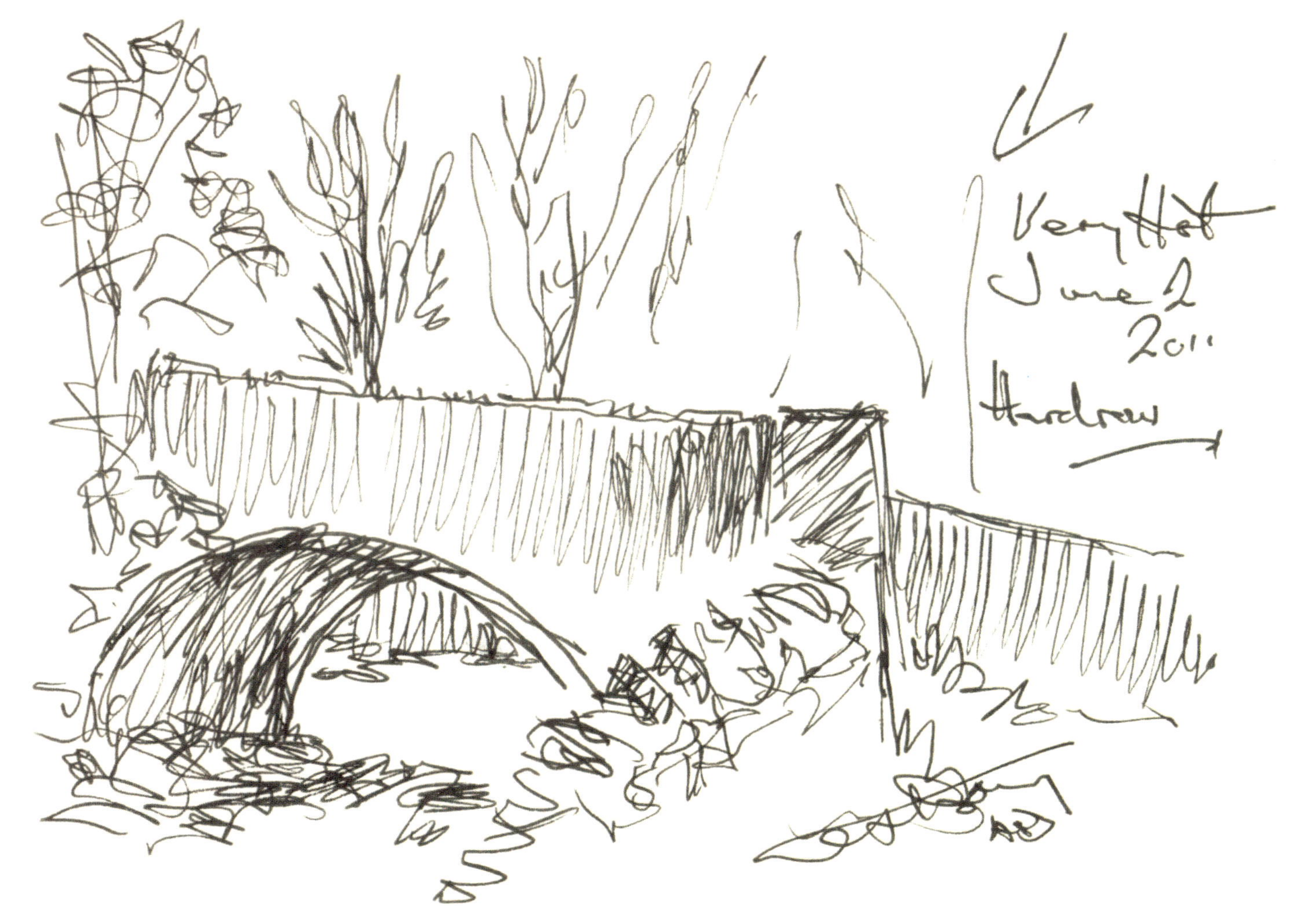
Very Hot
June 2
2011
Hardraw

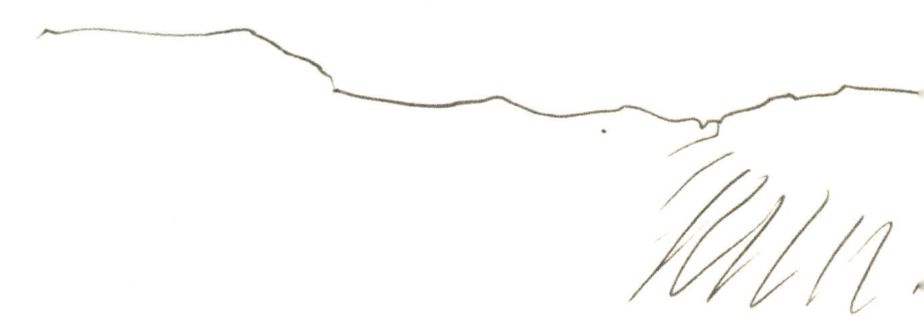

Kilnsey Crag

Wharfedale at this location is quite a wide, flat valley; Kilnsey Crag comes in from the left, dominating the landscape. Coming from the direction of Kettlewell, you can see the Lion's Head, with the rock overhang forming its chin. It amazes me to see climbers gripping to this overhang in pursuit of adrenaline.

Wharfedale Kilnsey Aug 2004

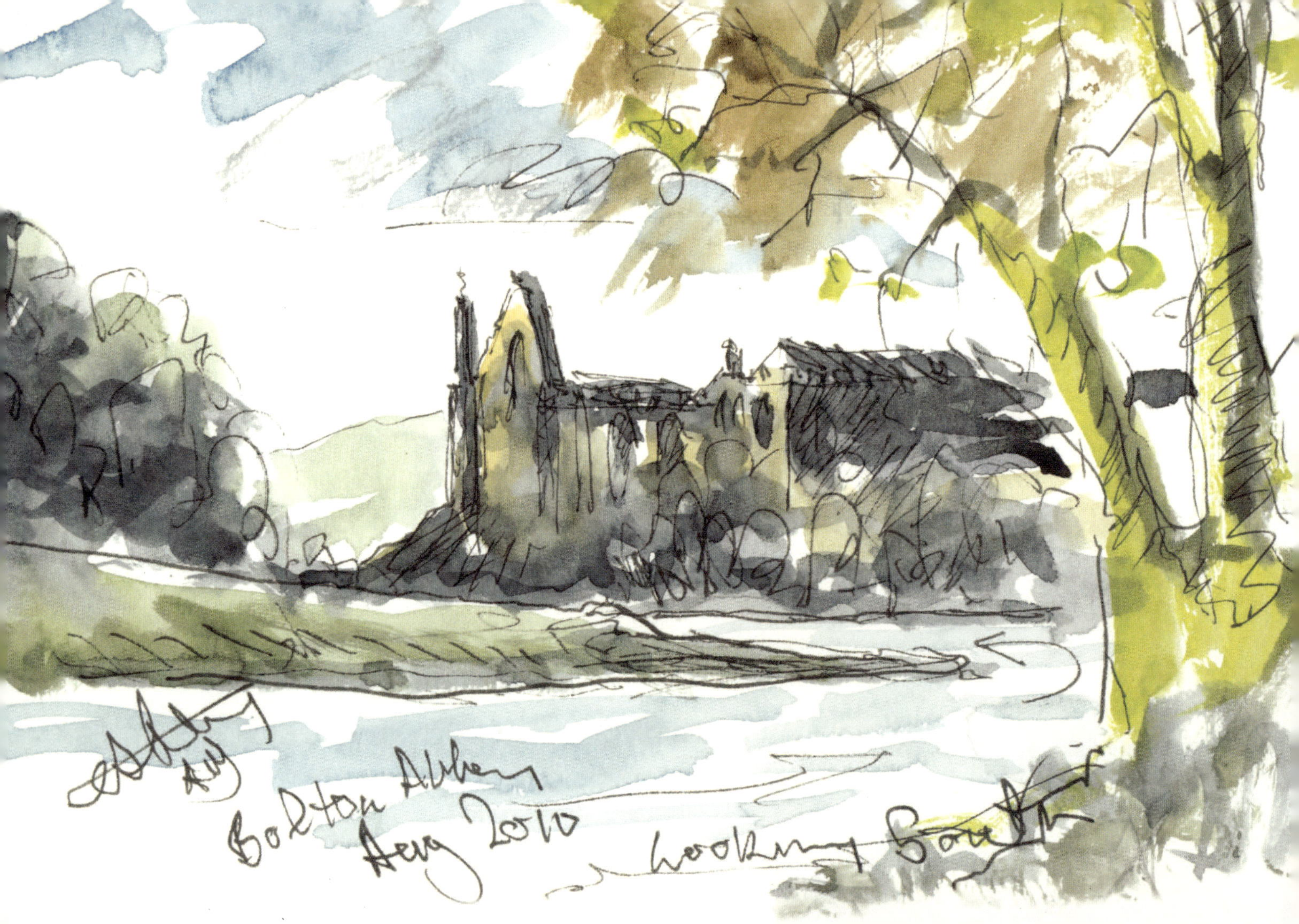
Bolton Abbey
Aug 2010
Looking South

Bolton Abbey (left)

Situated on the river Wharfe Bolton Abbey is another location of Turner and Thomas Girtin. Girtin died in his early twenties and, hearing of his death, Turner commented “Had Tom Girtin lived I should have starved” — such was the strength of Girtin’s paintings. Both artists are favourites of mine as they both had skill and passion.

Castle Bolton (below)

I was first made aware of Castle Bolton by the artist Fred Lawson, who every month wrote a feature called ‘Letter from the Dales’. Turner came up to Yorkshire and also painted Castle Bolton; I worked with Welcome to Yorkshire to inspire others to follow in the Yorkshire footsteps of Turner — and the Turner Trail was created.

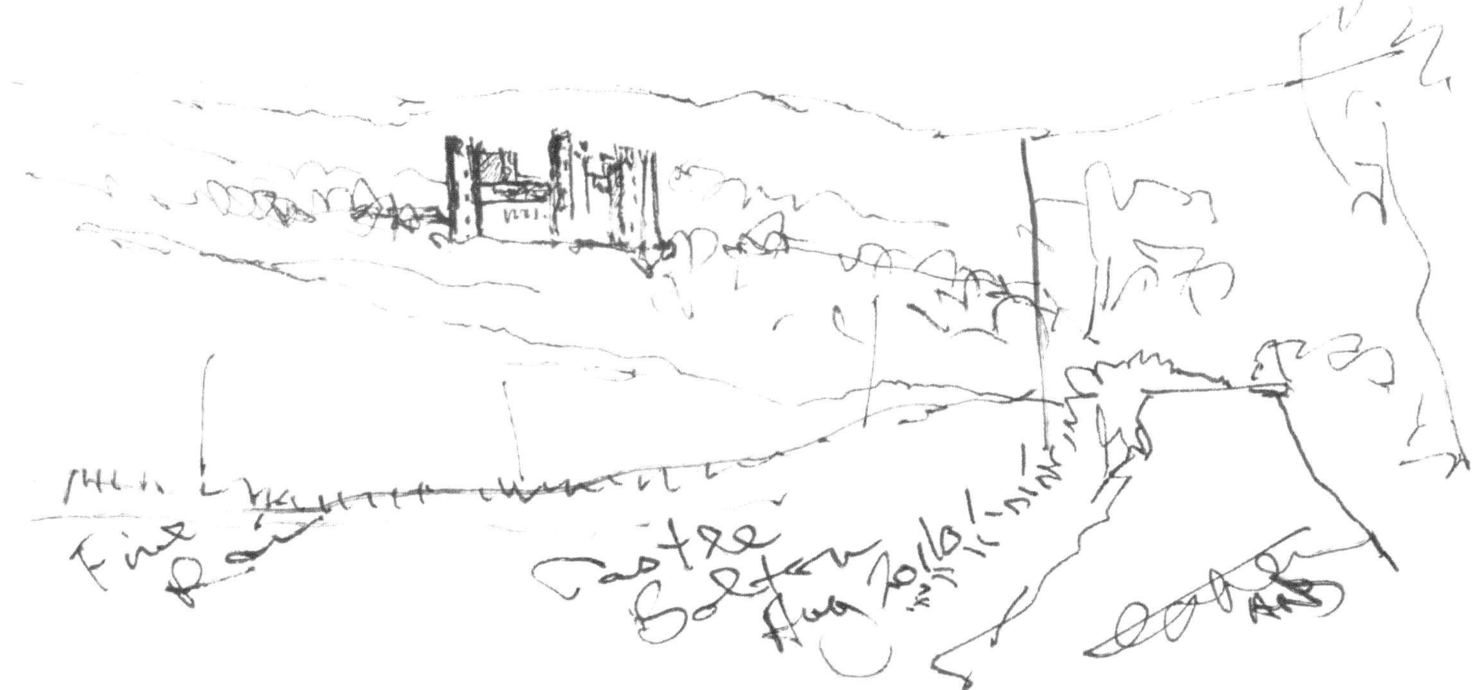

Road to Hubberholme

What I love about this area is how the barns nestle into the valley in upper Wharfedale, which is slightly different from Swaledale where there appears to be a barn in every field. I love the intertwining fells coming down in to the valley like huge mammals sleeping cheek to jowl, sharing the space available.

Colours are important,
they put life into the
landscape
and give it its depth
So that your eyes will
read what she, the landscape.
is trying to say to you.
This is her love letter to you
I Believe if we could all read
what she is trying to say to us
we would all look after her
Much more than we say we do.
We don't own her, she's here all the time.
it is we who only stay a while
No one man should own a Mountain,
We are only the keepers of Mother Earth
it is not ours But for the next
generation in life to follow on

Alan Jackson 1997

(1)

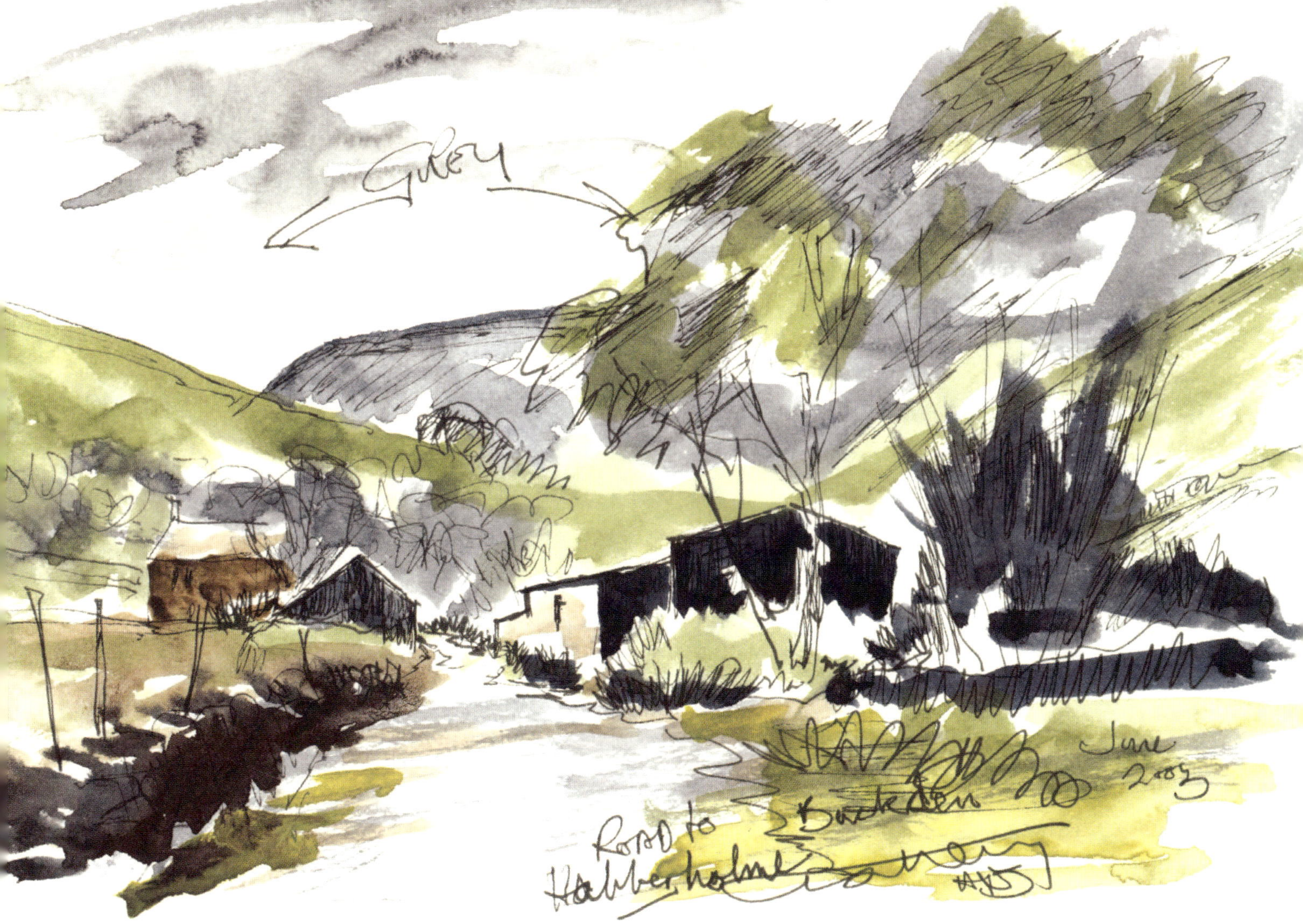
GREY
June 2003
Buckden
Road to Hubberholme

LIGHT

West Nab 1st July 2004

ANJ

West Nab from Saddleworth Moor looking towards Holmfirth

This is one fell you can see from the M62 motorway. Like a saddle it connects with Deer Hill at the other end, which is not included in this sketch. I felt that the wooden fence was dancing across the moor, with its function to keep sheep in and people out long forgotten.

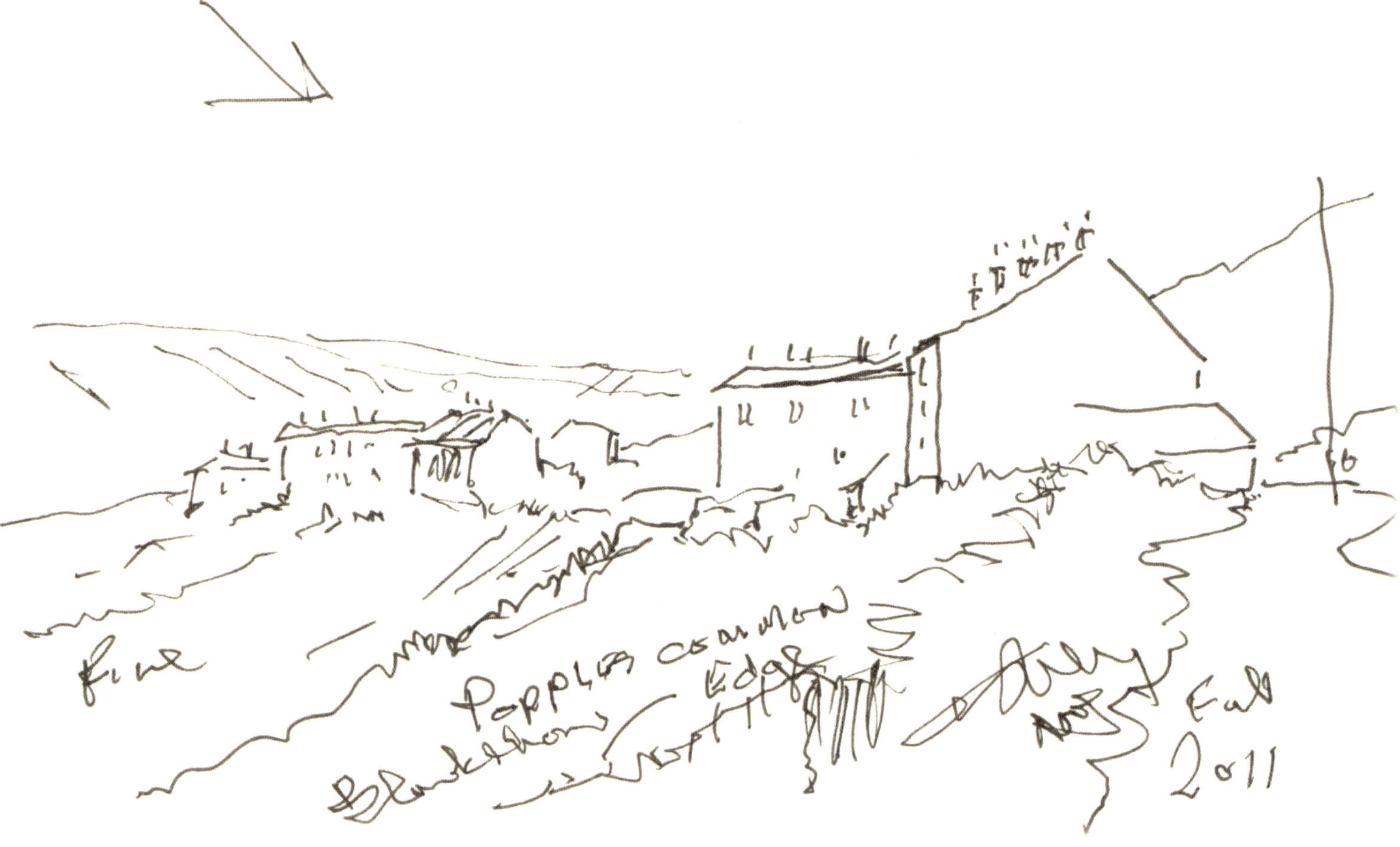
common
Edge
Blackthorn
Fall
2011

Popples Common - Blackshaw Edge

This is real West Riding gritstone country. The Bulldog of Yorkshire, Sir Bernard Ingham, originates from Hebden Bridge. He typifies everything that Yorkshire Grit stands for. I always feel this area conjures up the atmosphere of the Brontës as it is both wild and beautiful. Haworth is only a stone's throw away.

Slippery Stones (overleaf)

I have known this moor from boyhood, when pals and I would hike over Margery Hill onto Cut Gate and down into the big valley of the Derwent, where we'd have our sandwiches with a bottle of pop, then take off our clothes and go for a swim, even on a misty day. Keeping our eye out for the moorland wardens, we'd dry off with the wind and the sun — we never thought to take towels. We'd then walk over the moor with the dusk turning to darkness, seeing the Flouch Inn, lights shining like glow worms on the horizon. Then from the Flouch, we'd catch a bus to Barnsley and home. As a boy I tried to hold the imprint the image in my head and then reproduce it in my sketchbook when I returned home; it was to train my memory for later landscapes.

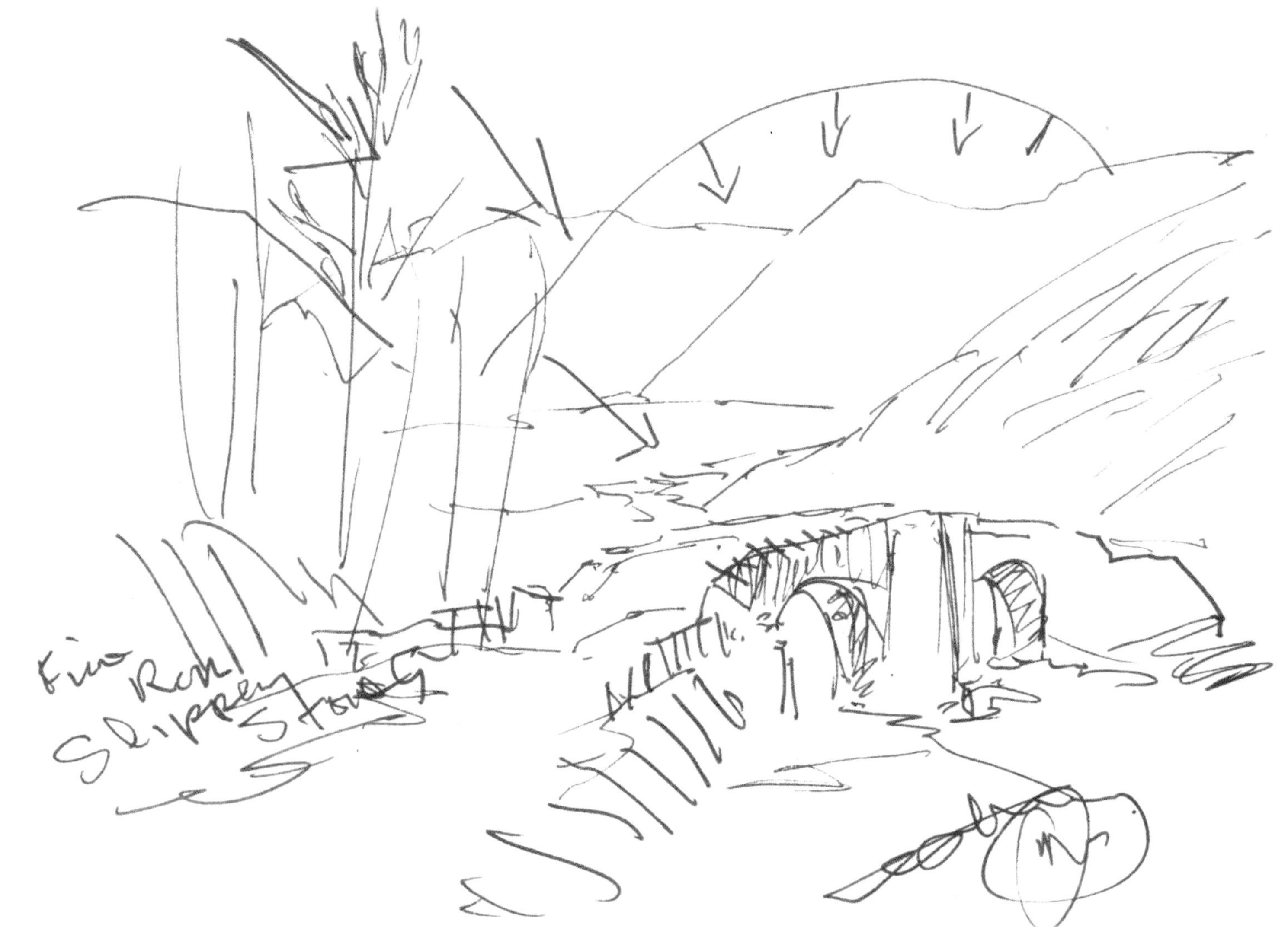
Fine Rock
Slippery
Stones

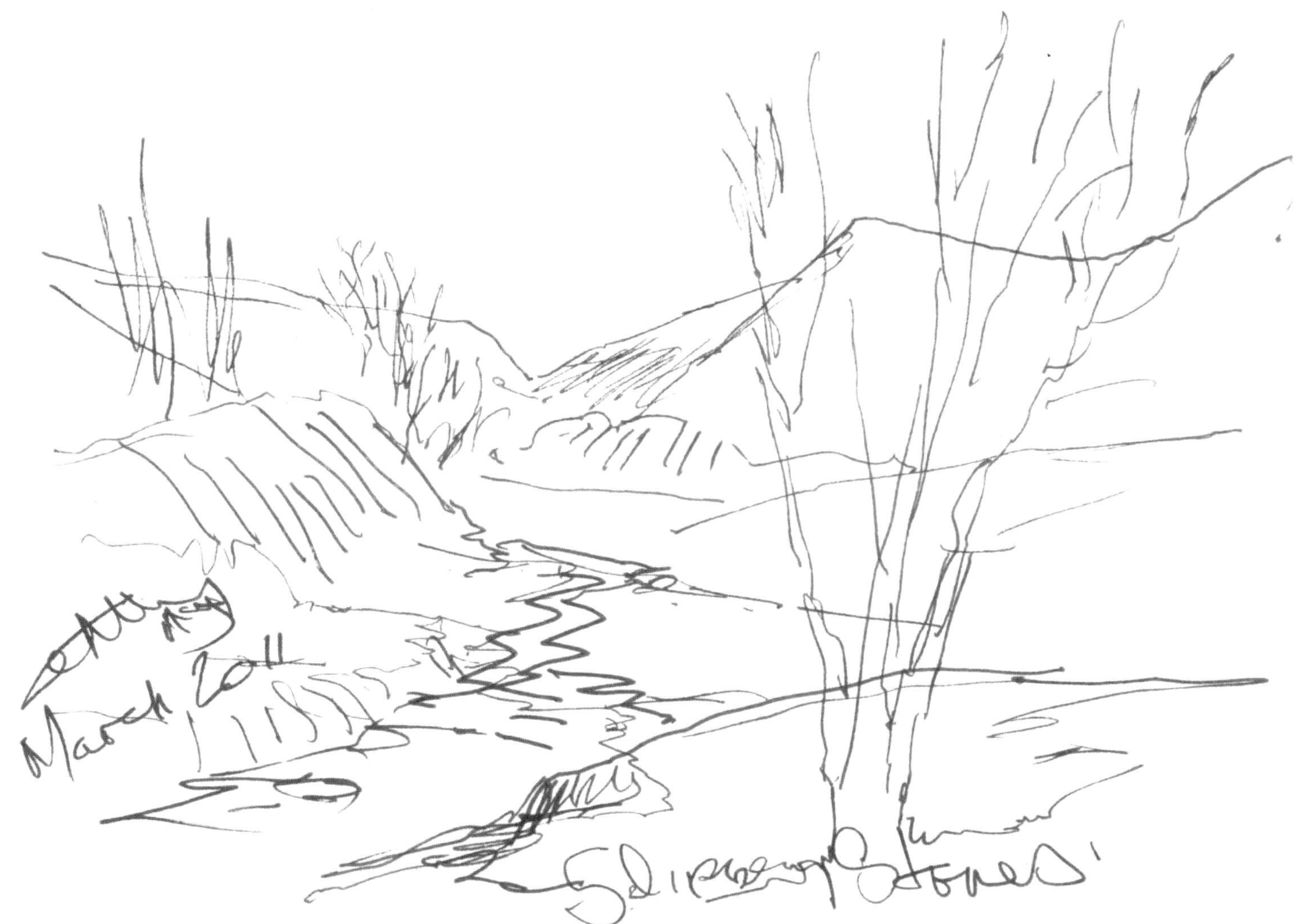

March 2011
'Slippery Stones'

Nont's Road above Huddersfield

In the distance is Nont Sarah's, another isolated inn that is happy to welcome the moorland lover. Nont is a lovely Yorkshire word meaning 'aunt'. From here you will have a 'wow' view of the moors. I tend to have a soup and sandwich at local inns when I am out sketching, as to feed the heart one must first feed the stomach.

One must never give up
Although some people would like to see you giving up.
to be a painter is easy
to be an Artist is a great gift
The painter just paints pictures,
But the Artist puts his soul into his paintings.
So the painter gives you a picture
And the Artist gives the world a painting
Ashley Jackson 1968

Norris Road

6.15pm

Sun to set.

Blakey Ridge

I remember Blakey Ridge in 1963 when I did the Lyke Wake Walk. It was 22nd November — the day President Kennedy was assassinated. I was introduced to this outdoor life by my good friend and boss Ron Darwent, and I shall be forever grateful. Sadly he passed away recently, but he will will not be forgotten when I walk upon these moors.

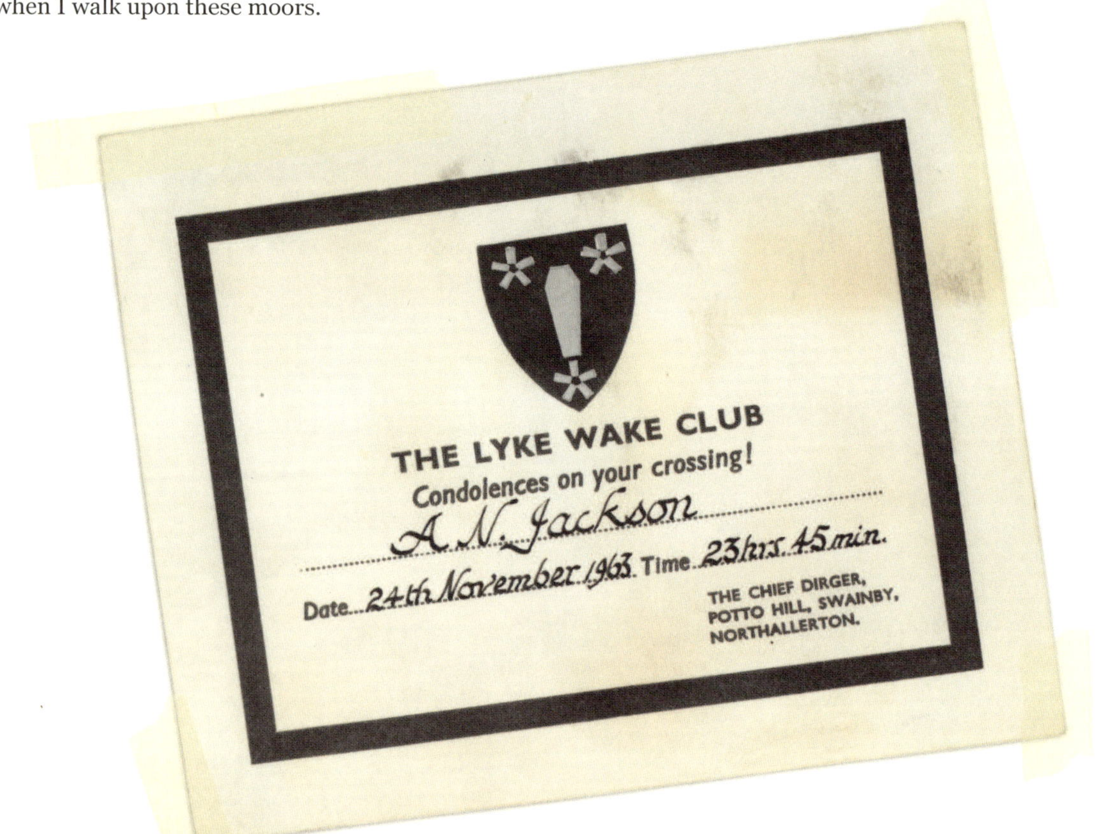

THE LYKE WAKE CLUB

Condolences on your crossing!

A. N. Jackson

Date 24th November 1963 Time 23hrs 45min.

THE CHIEF DIRGER,
POTTO HILL, SWAINBY,
NORTHALLERTON.

Blakey
Ridge
18.9.2009

Great Shunner Fell

From the village of Hardraw you can see Great Shunner Fell, the third highest mountain in the Yorkshire Dales, a majestic view where the river cuts through the fells. The Pennine Way passes over its summit, with a paved path to prevent erosion of the peat, on the way from Hawes to Keld.

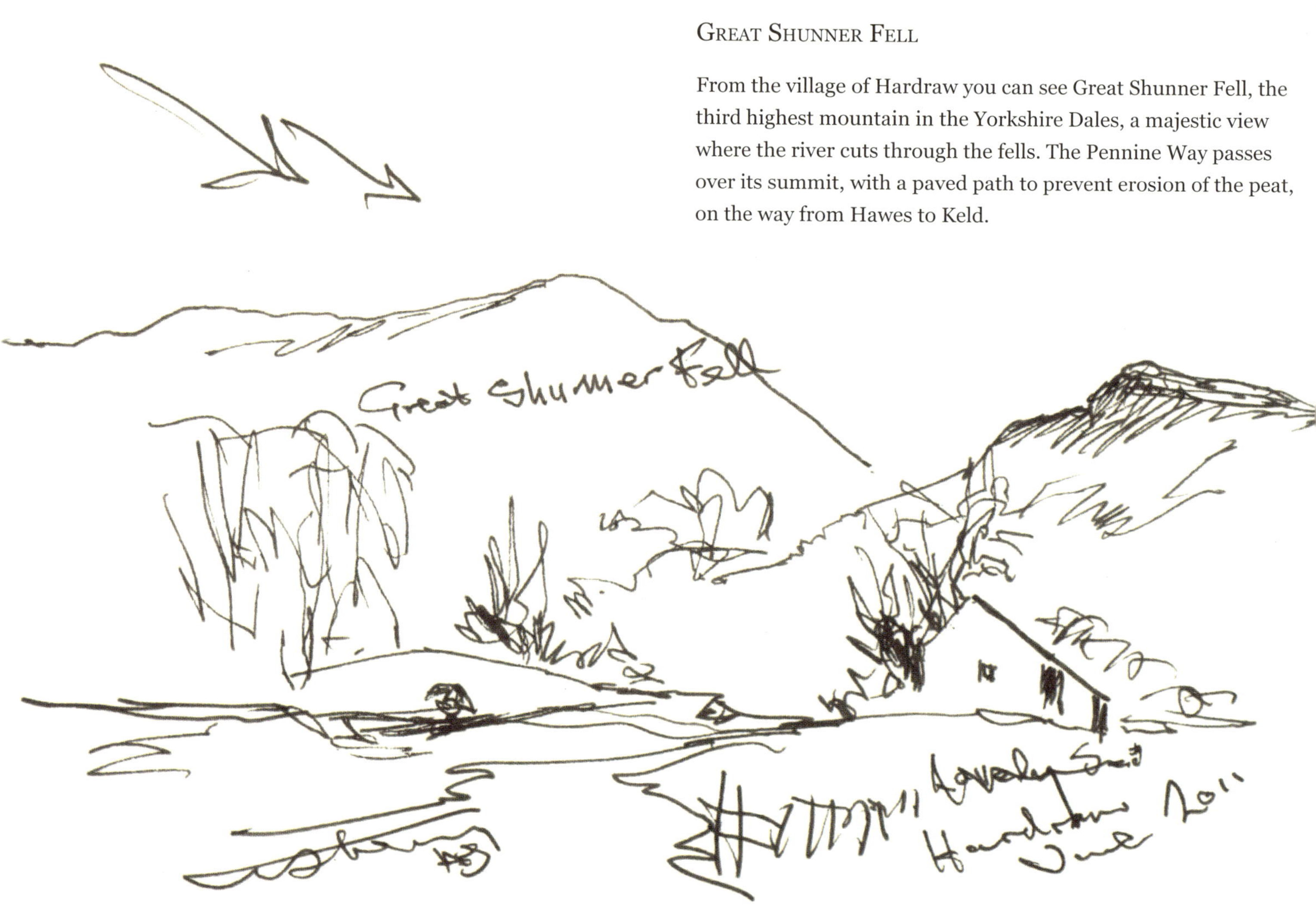

Garsdale Head

Here you can see Ribblehead Viaduct in the mid-distance. It is a homage to Victorian engineering and architecture, and the bloody-mindedness of those who assisted in its construction, bridging the valley and cutting across this unforgiving moor.

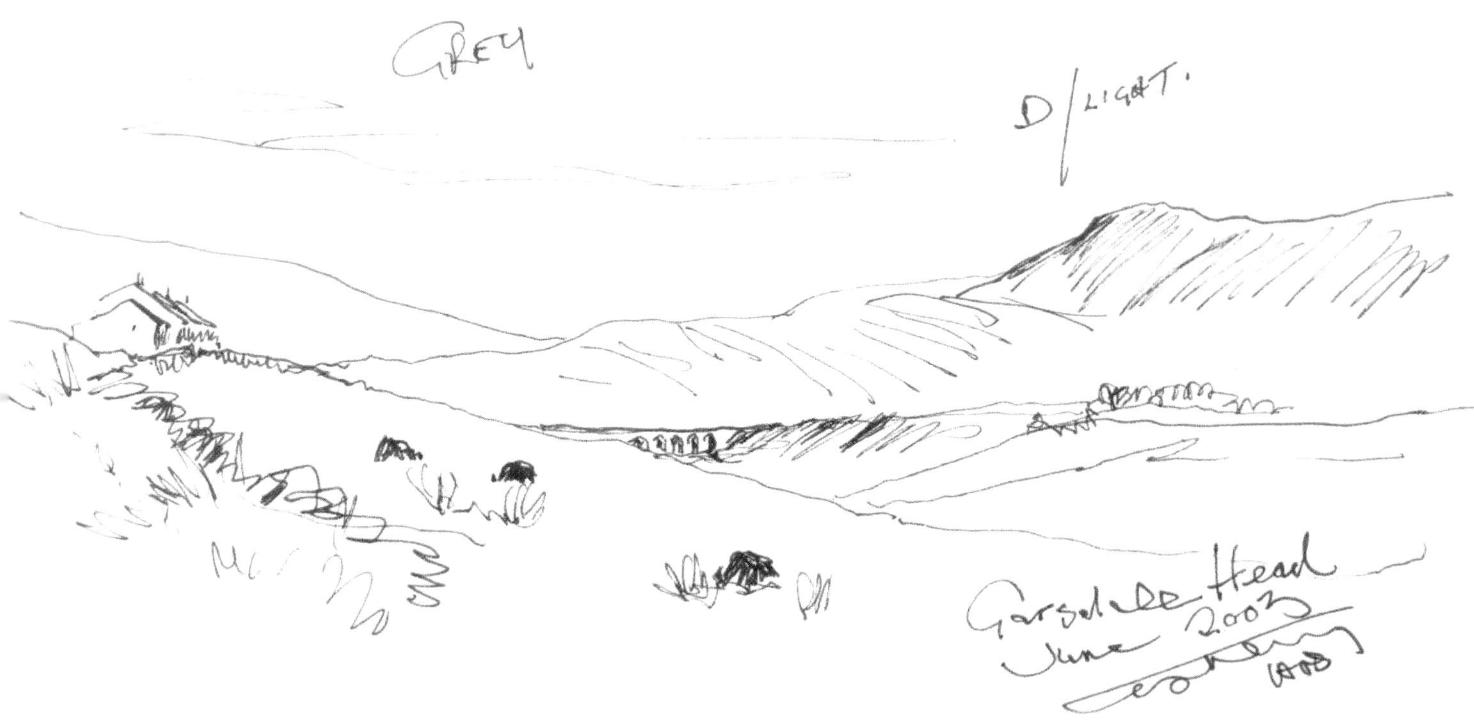

Emley Moor from Saddleworth Moor with West Nab in the distance

The snow had fallen and it was extremely cold, but what remained was a clear day with a biting frost on exposed skin. Oh for a drop of the hard stuff to warm the soul — and fingers, of course. It reminds me of a quote in one of my old sketchbooks; reproduced opposite.

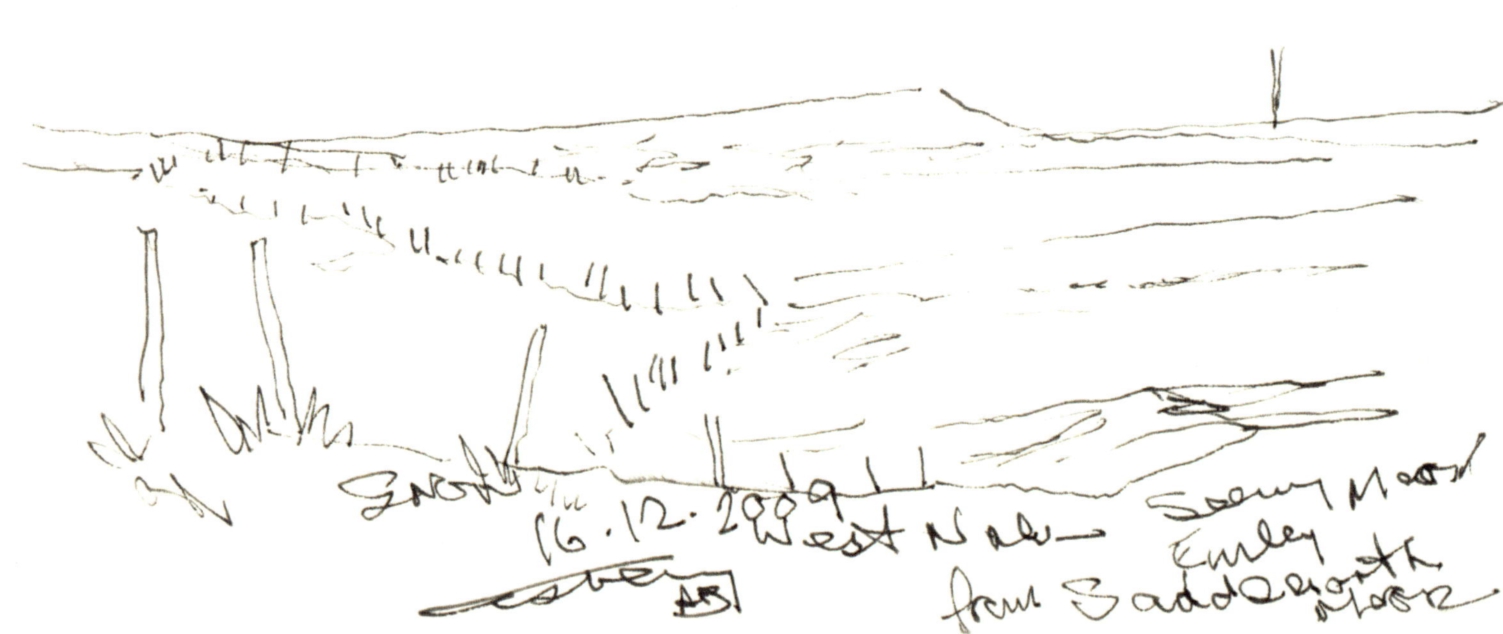

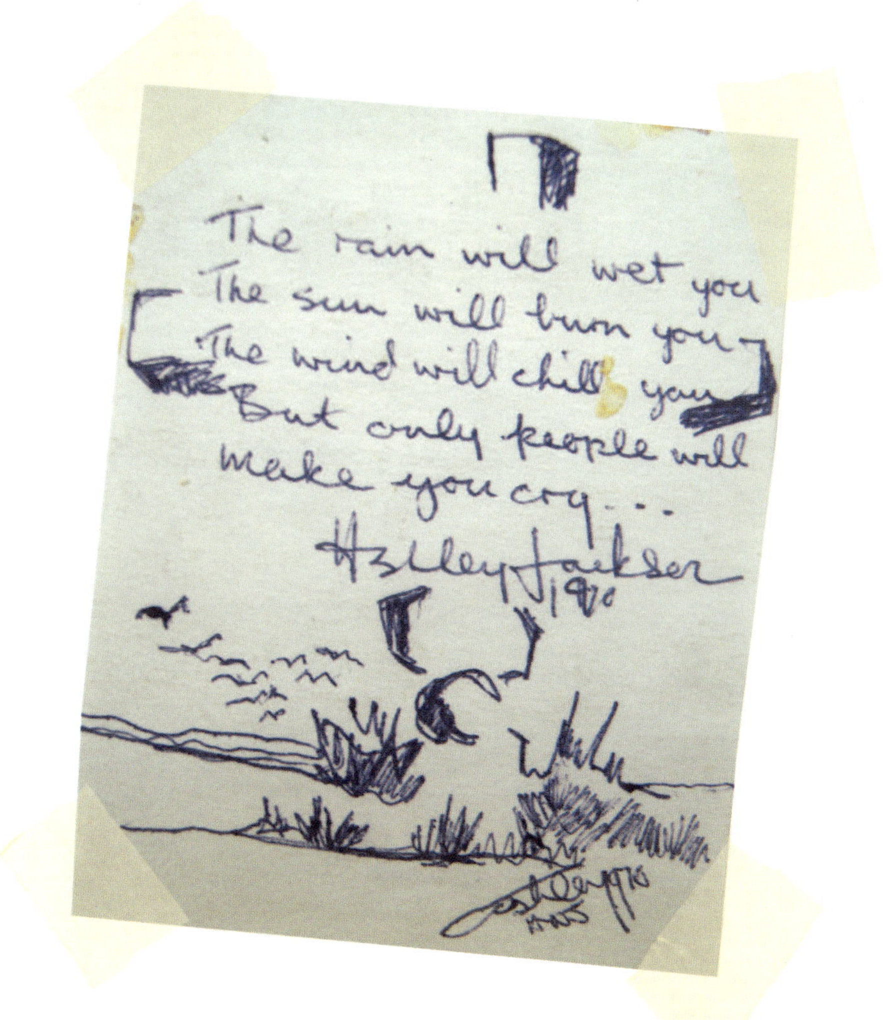

The rain will wet you
The sun will burn you
The wind will chill you
But only people will
make you cry...

Ashley Jackson
1970

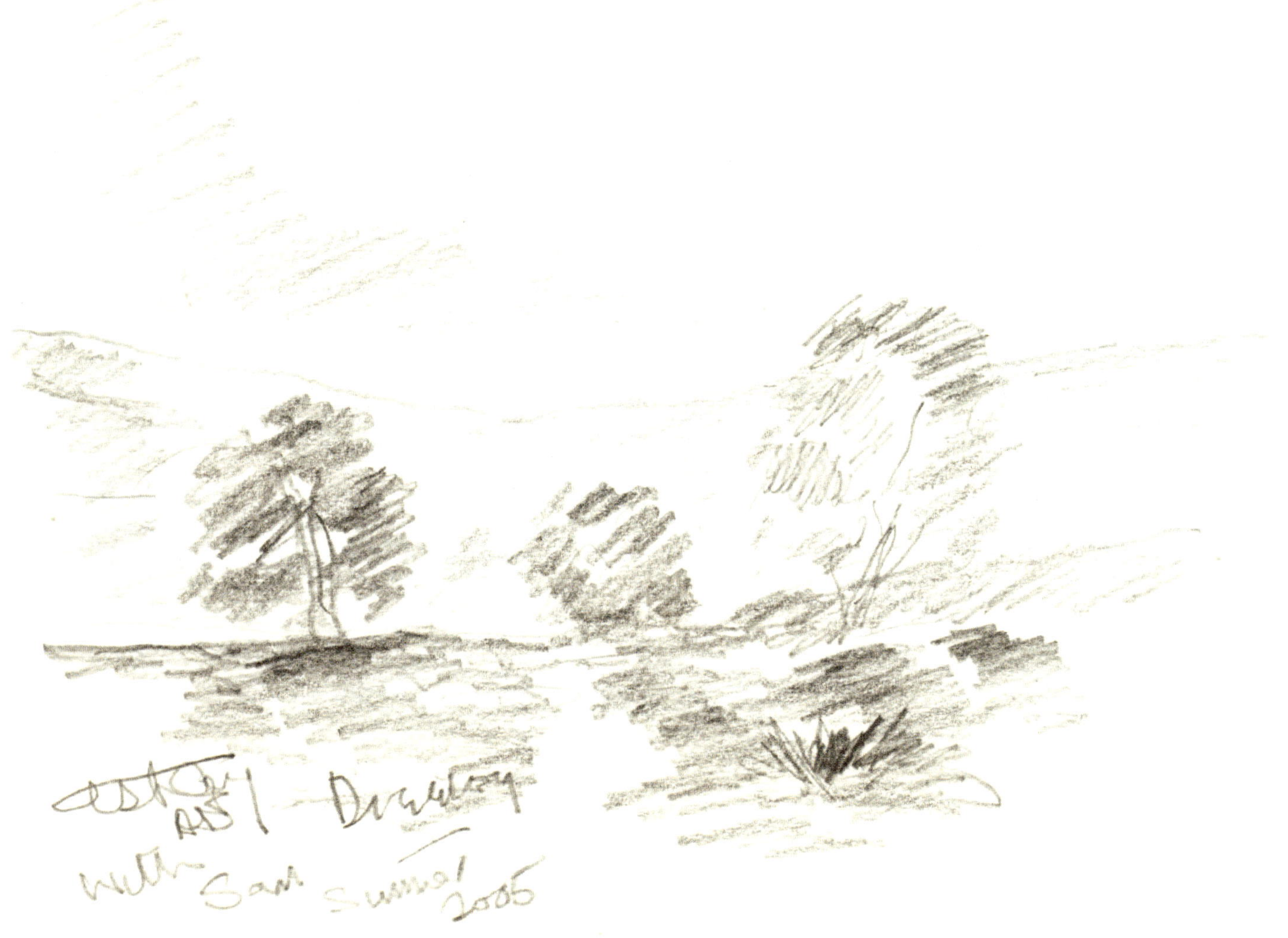
Drawing
with Sam
Summer 2005

Digley (left)

One of my favourite walks around the Holme Valley, although don't go on a weekend as you will look like you are on a pilgrimage, such is its popularity. I know that I am purely selfish in wishing to indulge in my isolation, but I love to go when all the herds have gone home.

Whitens Moor (overleaf)

I have always described the Yorkshire moors like frozen seas coming towards you whilst bustled in the swell. Here I felt that I was isolated on the great seas of the moors of Yorkshire; in the far distance you can see Stoodley Pike with Emley Moor on the left-hand side, both looking like sailing ships in the far distance. Like Turner I, too, wished to experience the nature of the sea and one early morning in January 1969 I went out in a fishing vessel out into the sea's graveyard.My wife had just given birth to our first child the previous November; as to be expected, she was not only upset for fear of losing me but cross for putting myself in danger.

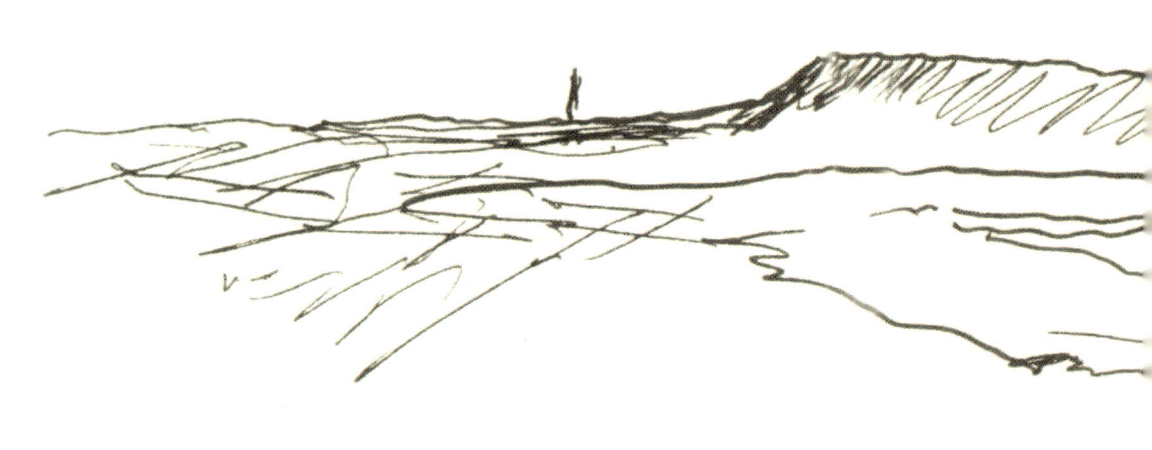

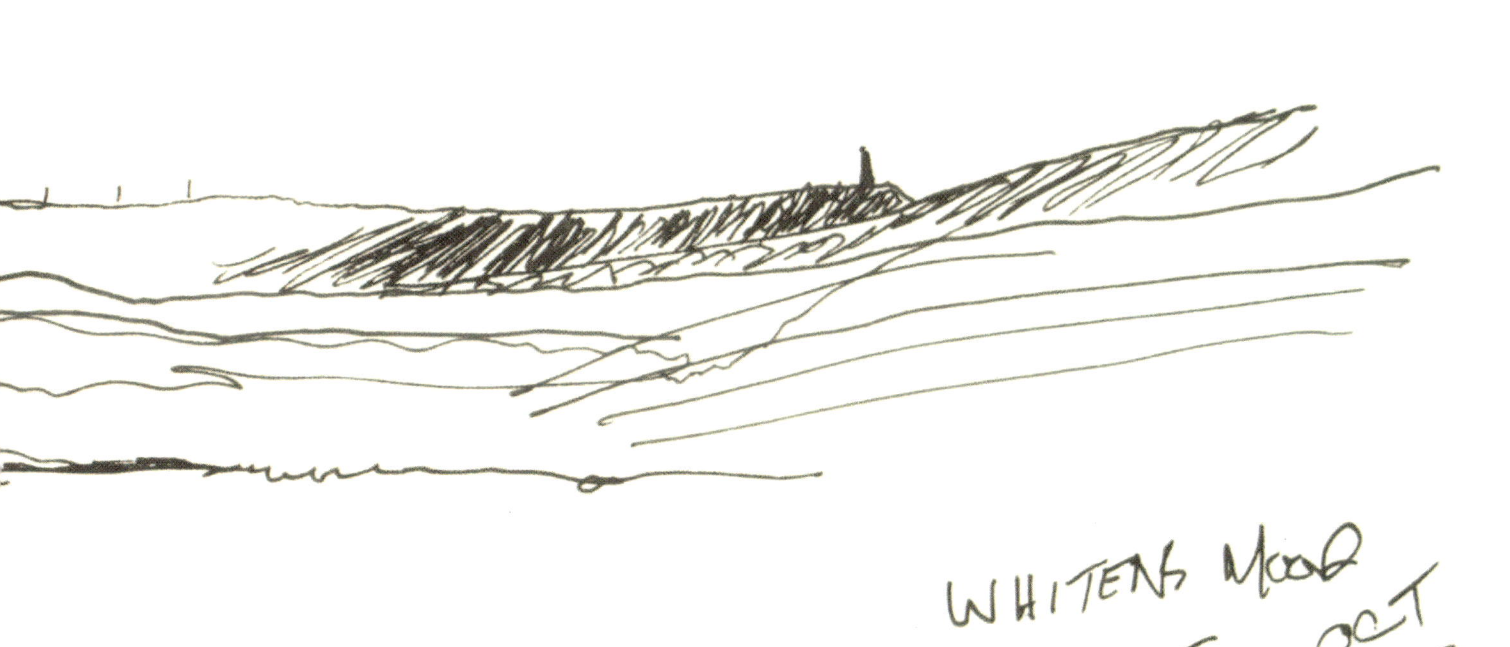
WHITENS MOOR
OCT
2003

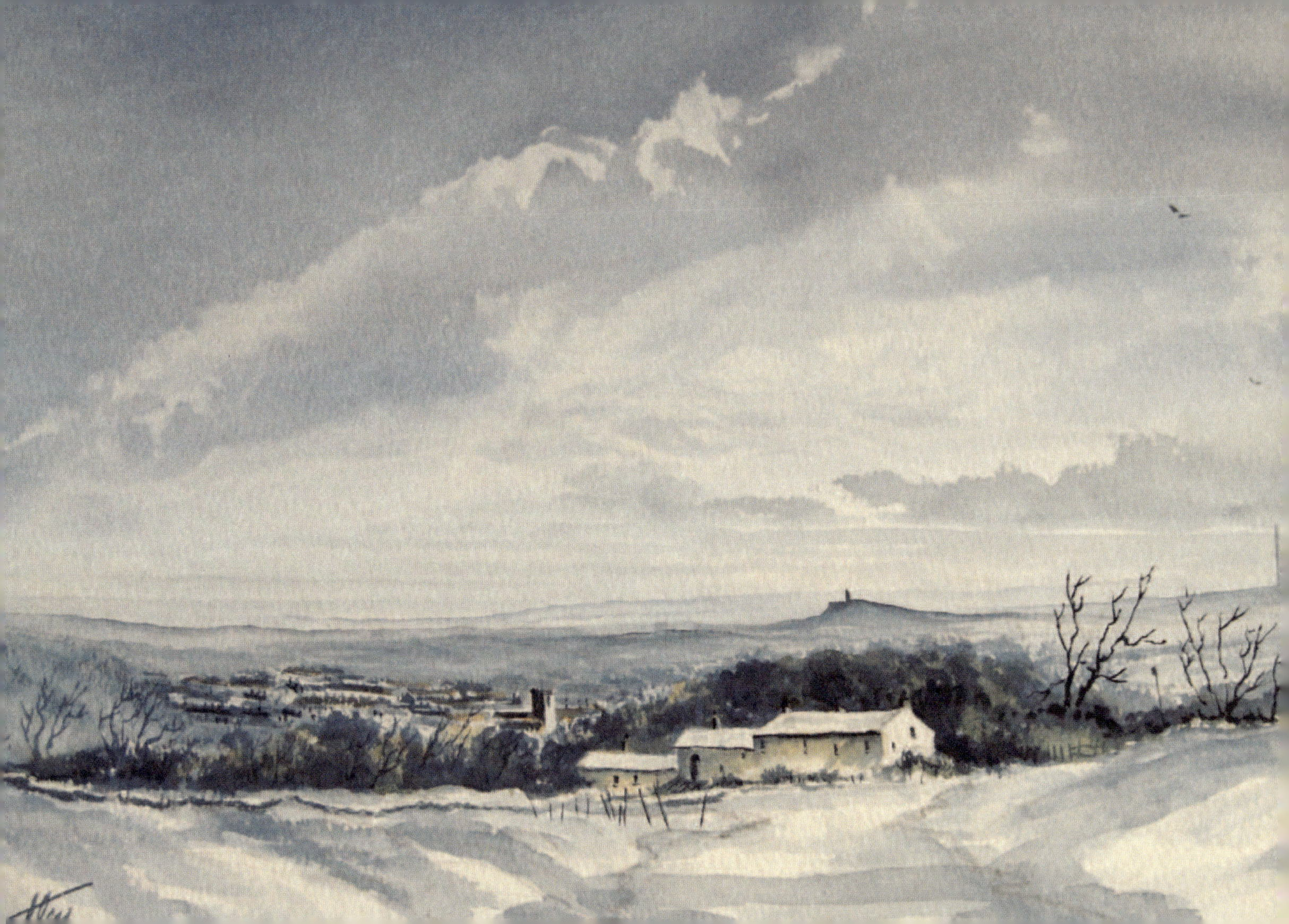

Meltham from West Nab

Looking down to Meltham from West Nab with the majestic monuments of Castle Hill and Emley Moor Mast standing proud against the skyline. It had a strong feeling of homecoming and community.

Halton Gill

The rain was light — what I would call 'graveyard rain' — causing a mist across the valley.

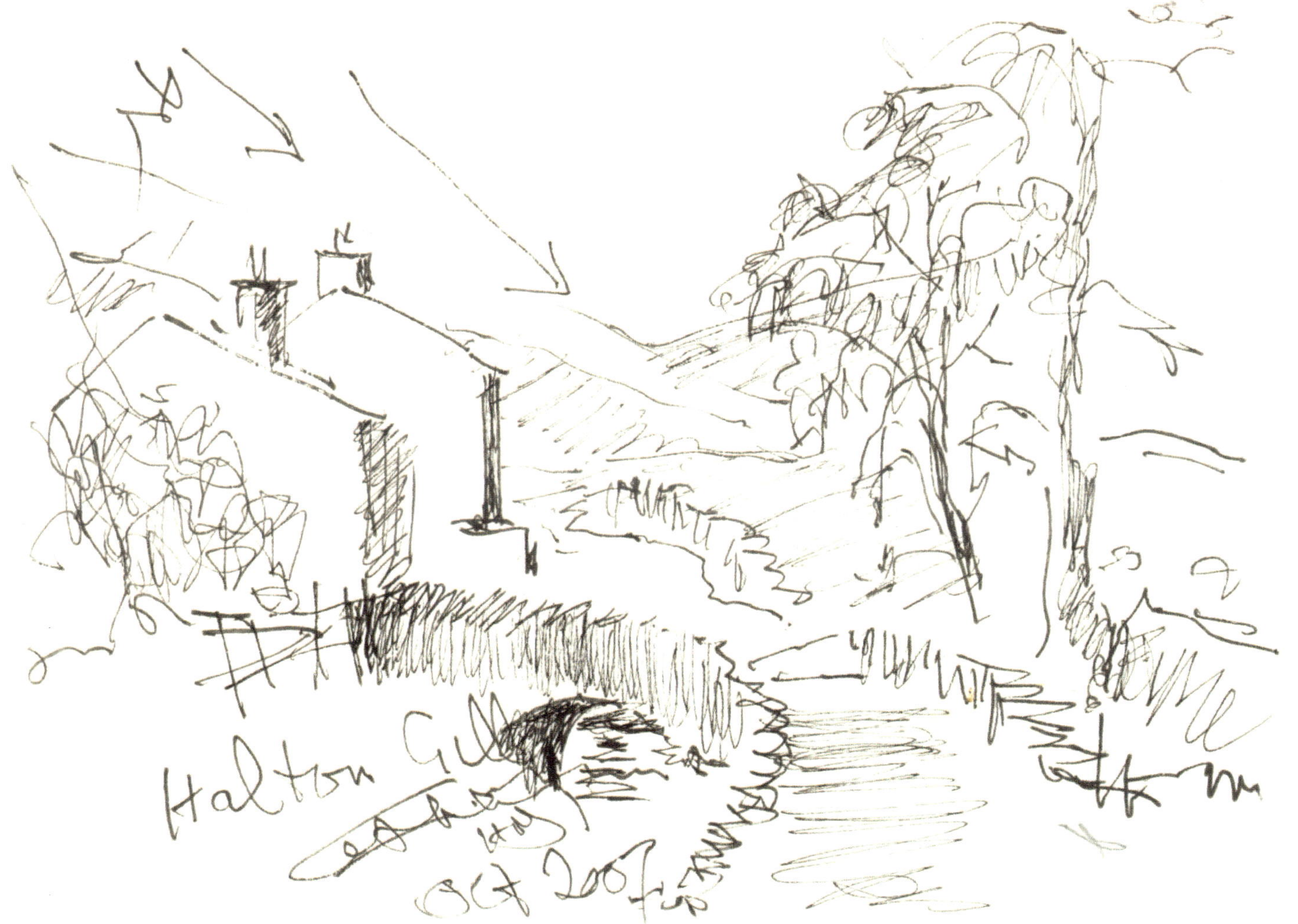
Halton Gill
Oct 2007

Ilkley Moor

I have had the great privilege of creating these pencil sketches on location, in the wind, rain, snow and occasional glimmer of sunshine. They represent a frozen moment in time, shared with Mother Nature. This could not be captured in a studio — it has to be felt.

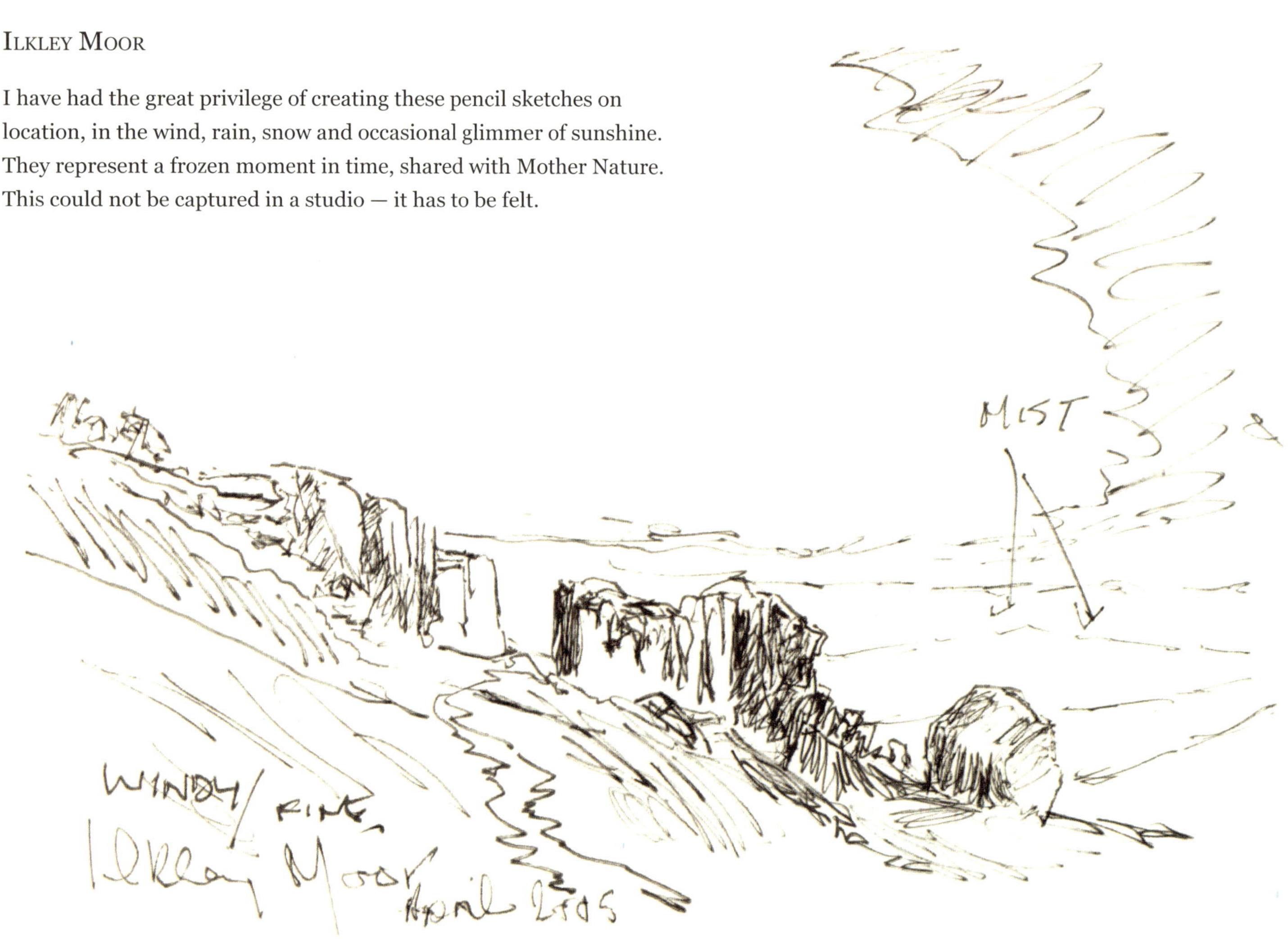

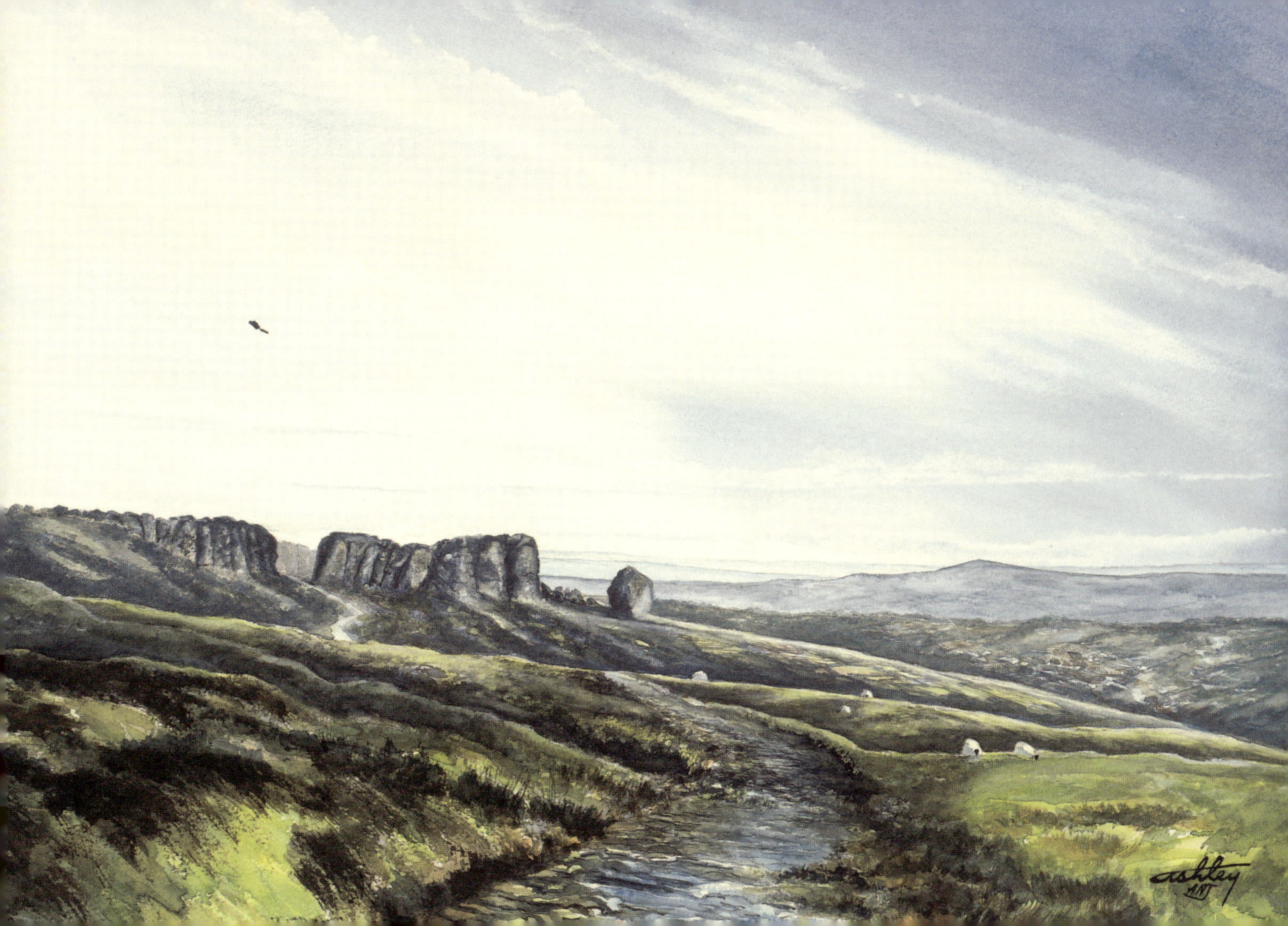
ashley

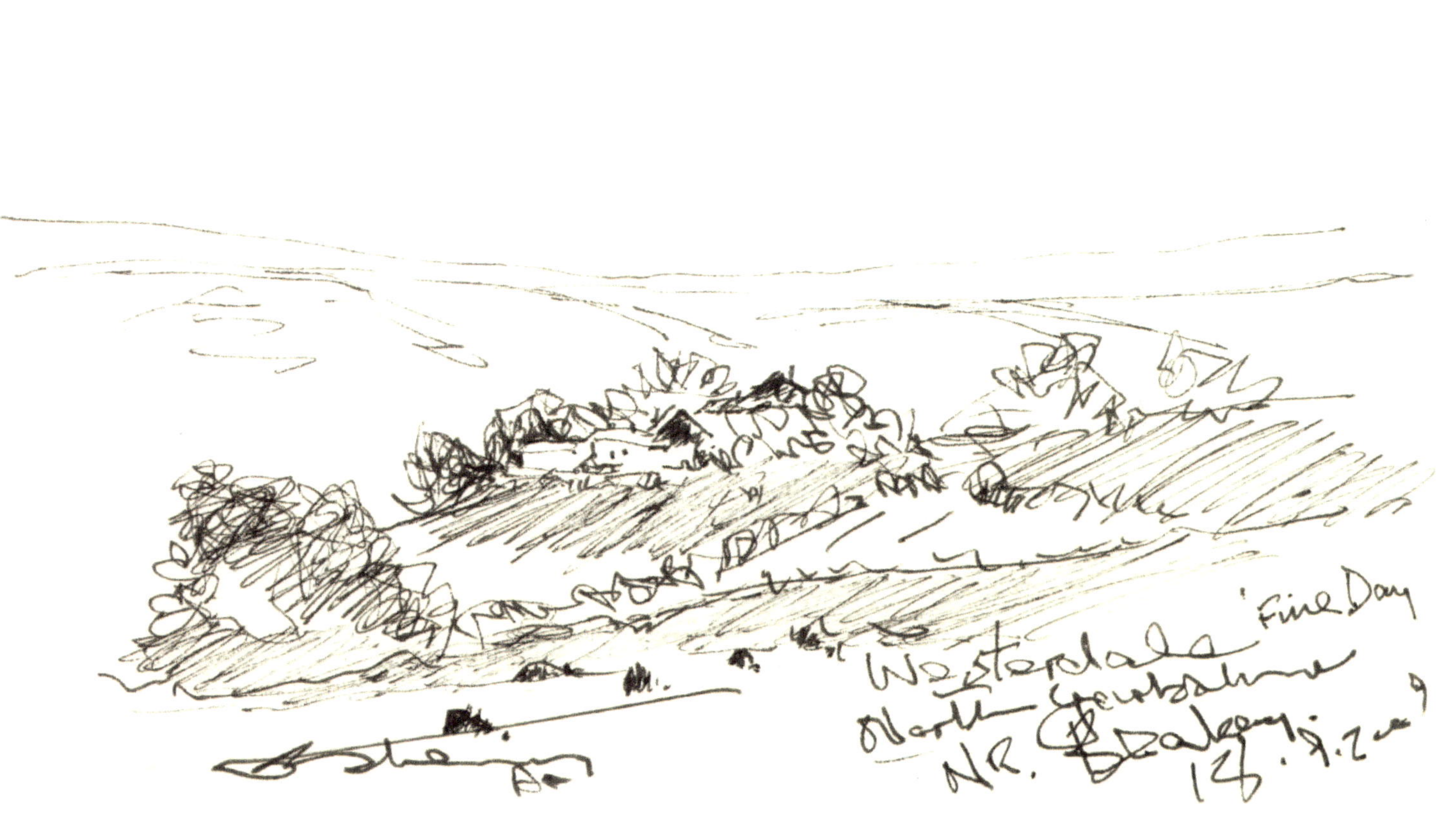
'Fine Day
Westerdale
North Yorkshire

Westerdale (left)

This was a fine day with the wind through my grey hair. I love to try to capture the farms nestling in the gullies of the moor and where the sky meets the horizon of the landscape; as a walker this sight gives you hope that you are nearing your journey's end.

Farndale Moor coming down from Blakey Ridge (overleaf)

Where you get pantiles on the roof instead of slate. The arrows are going up to meet the arrows coming down in the sky — this depicts the chinks of light coming through the sky.

Farndale

EAJ 18-9-2009

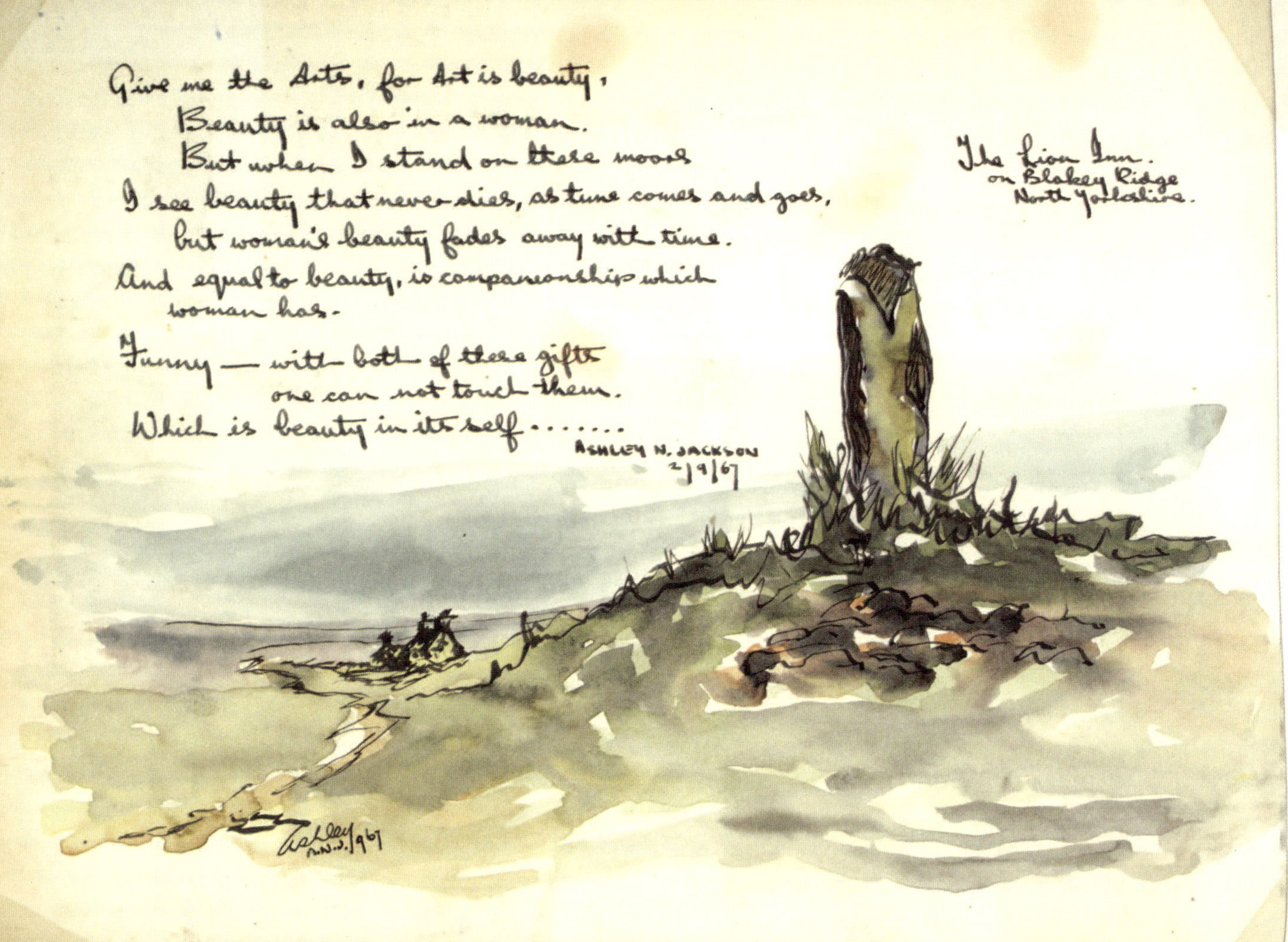
Give me the Arts, for Art is beauty,
Beauty is also in a woman.
But when I stand on these moors
I see beauty that never dies, as time comes and goes,
but woman's beauty fades away with time.
And equal to beauty, is companionship which
woman has.
Funny — with both of these gifts
one can not touch them.
Which is beauty in its self ....
ASHLEY N. JACKSON
2/9/67
The Lion Inn.
on Blakey Ridge
North Yorkshire.
Ashley
A.N.J. 1967

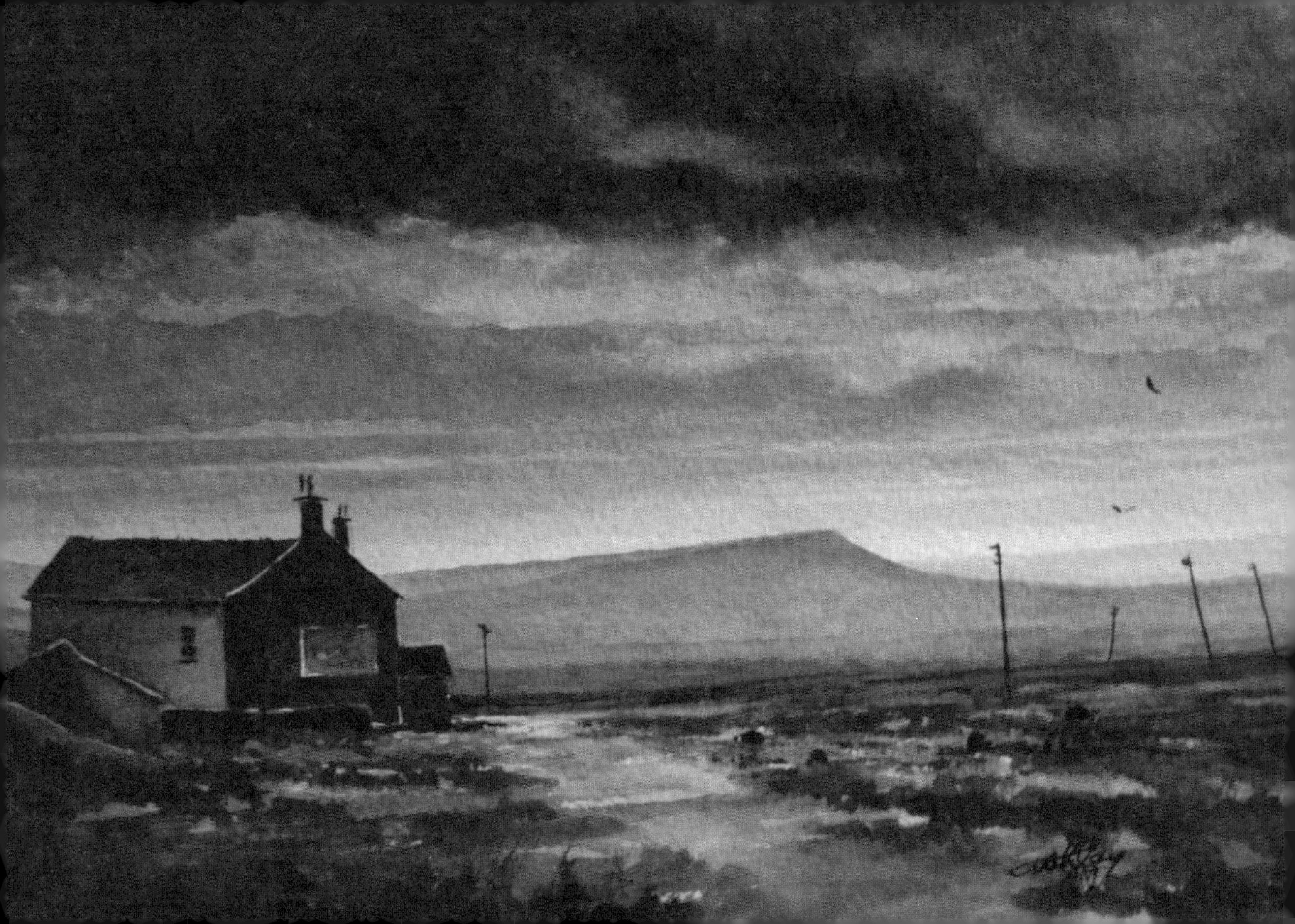

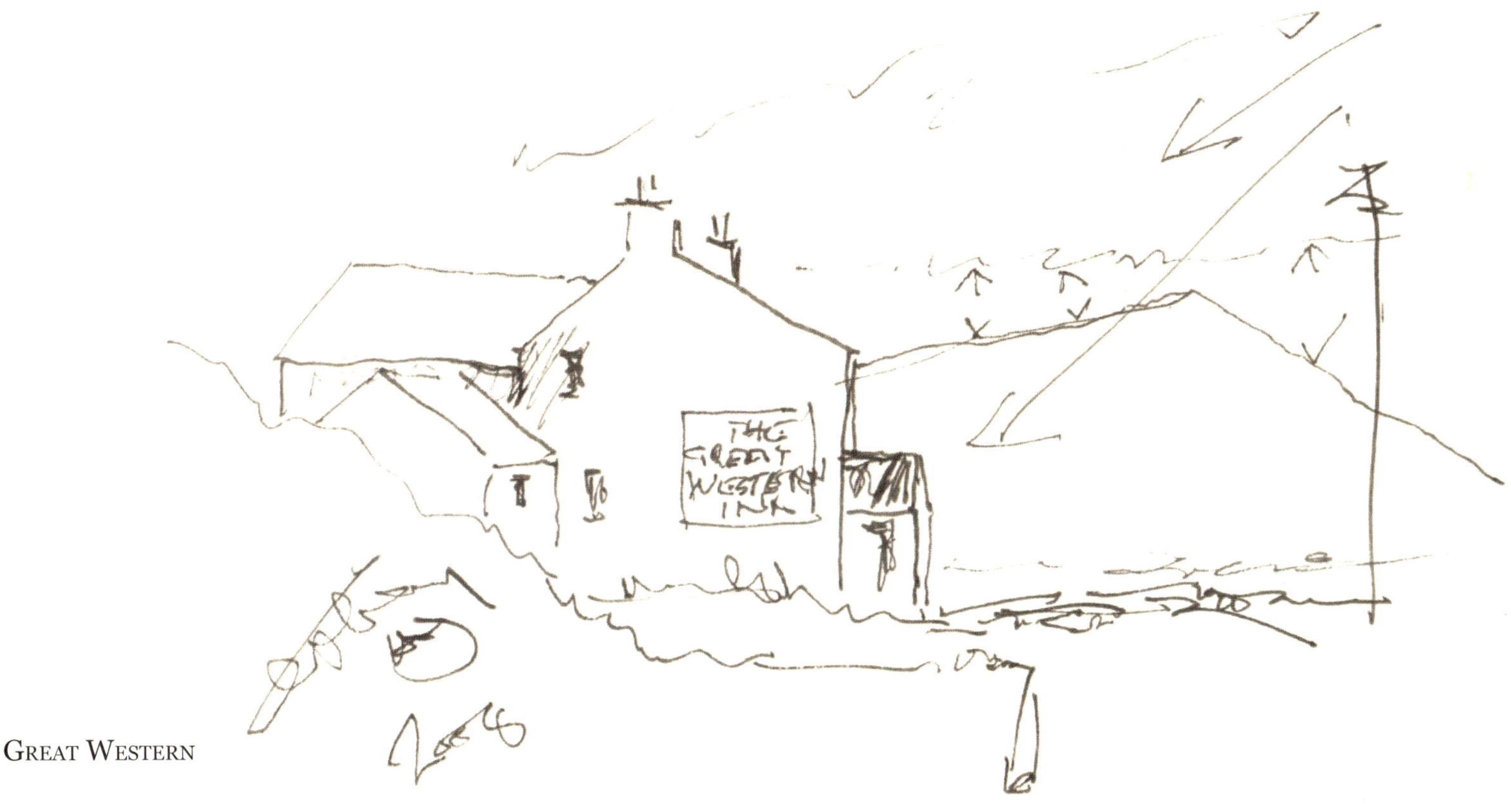

Great Western

Above Standedge Tunnel is isolated moorland where you can see West Nab in the distance. I love to paint the telegraph poles, to pattern the composition. Once standing and hearing some critics looking at my work in the West End of London when I was twenty-six, I heard one say to the other, “Jackson is getting very phallic, as time goes on, putting all these phallic symbols of telegraph poles”. If only they knew that the GPO, when putting up a new telegraph pole, did not take the old one down, and I had used them to my advantage.

Black Hill (facing page and overleaf)

I was privileged in my younger days to have drunk with the last landlady of the Isle of Skye Inn, Joan Bottomley. She lived in Holmfirth and on her retirement used to frequent the Elephant and Castle. She was one of Holmfirth's true characters, of which there are few remaining. Some of her pearls of wisdom have implanted in my soul. When I drew this sketch I thought of her and her husband surviving on this desolate landscape. Sadly the Water Board condemned the Isle of Skye for its sanitation seeping down into the reservoir. They did the same thing to the George and Dragon on the Woodhead road near Holmfirth. These were welcoming inns to the hardened walker — all gone, never to return.

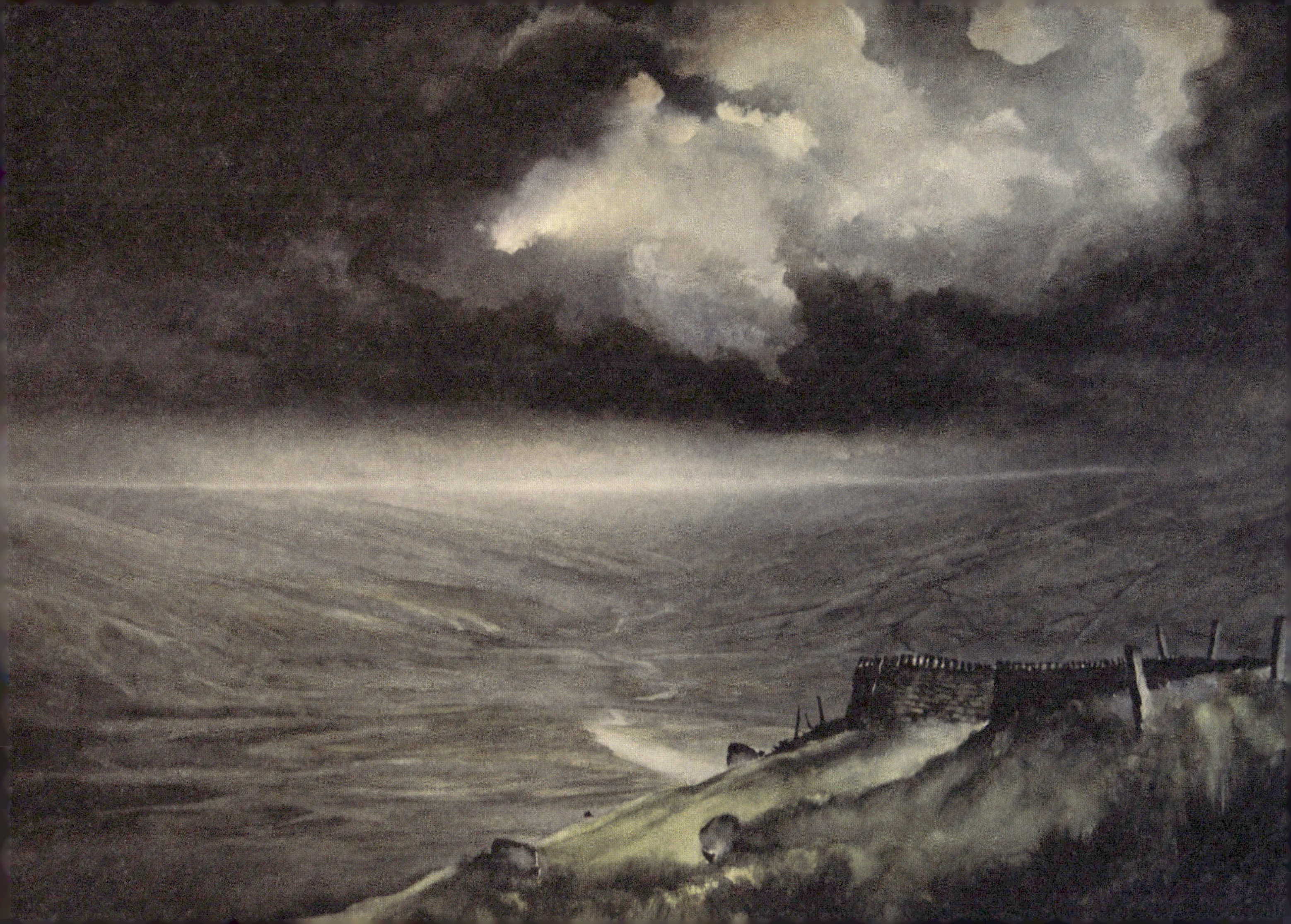

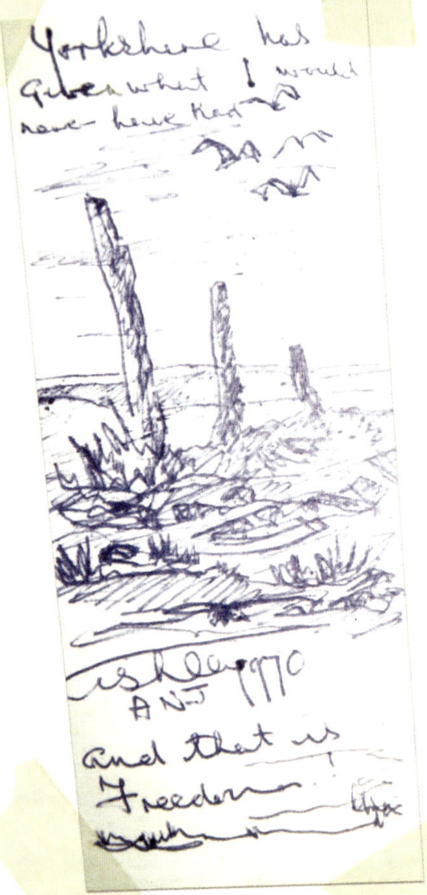

Yorkshire has
Given what I would
never have had

Ashley 1970
A N-J

And that is
Freedom

Mist
Windy
Snow

Isle o' Skye

Holme Moss

Holmfirth

16.12.2009

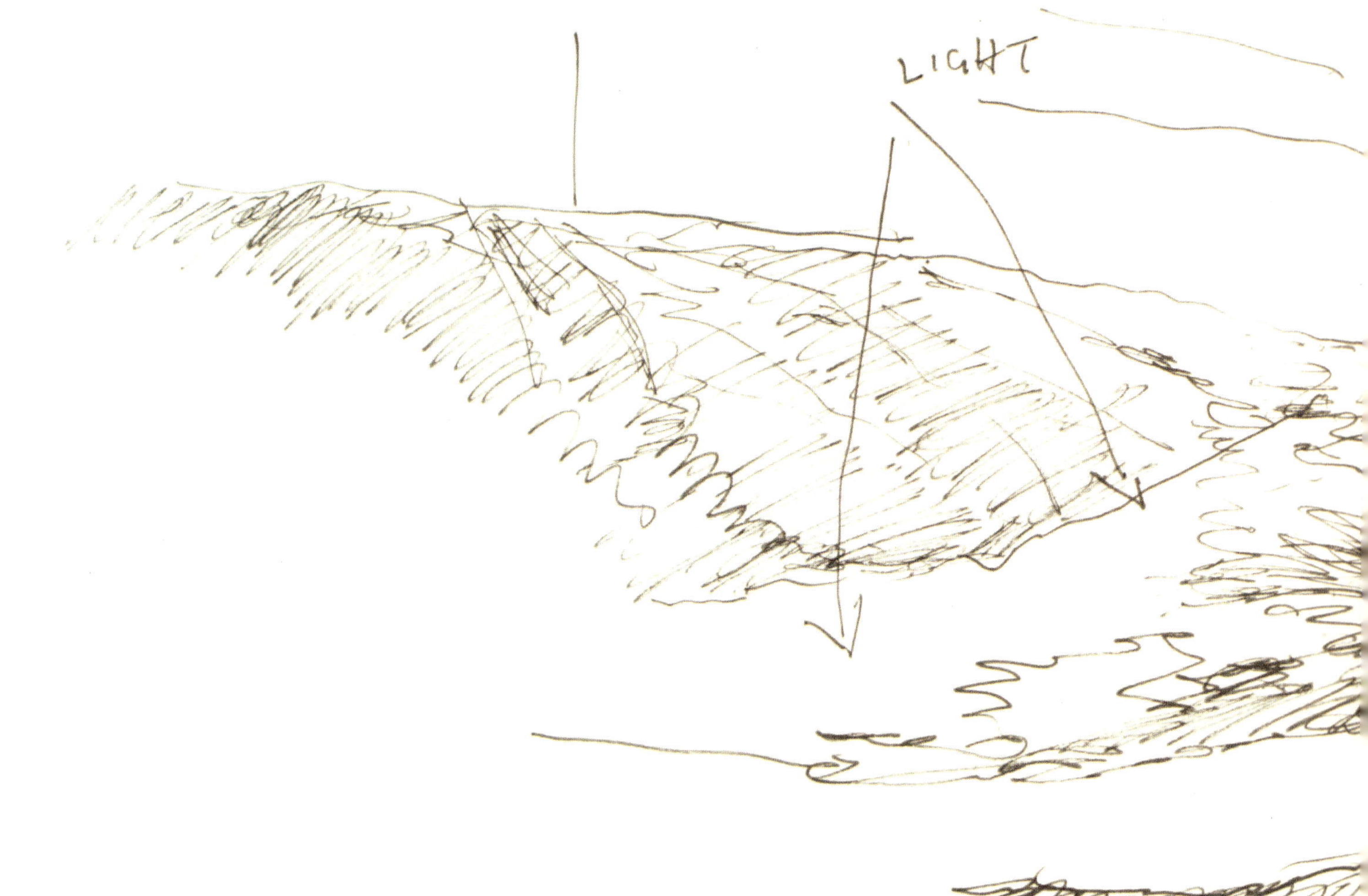
LIGHT

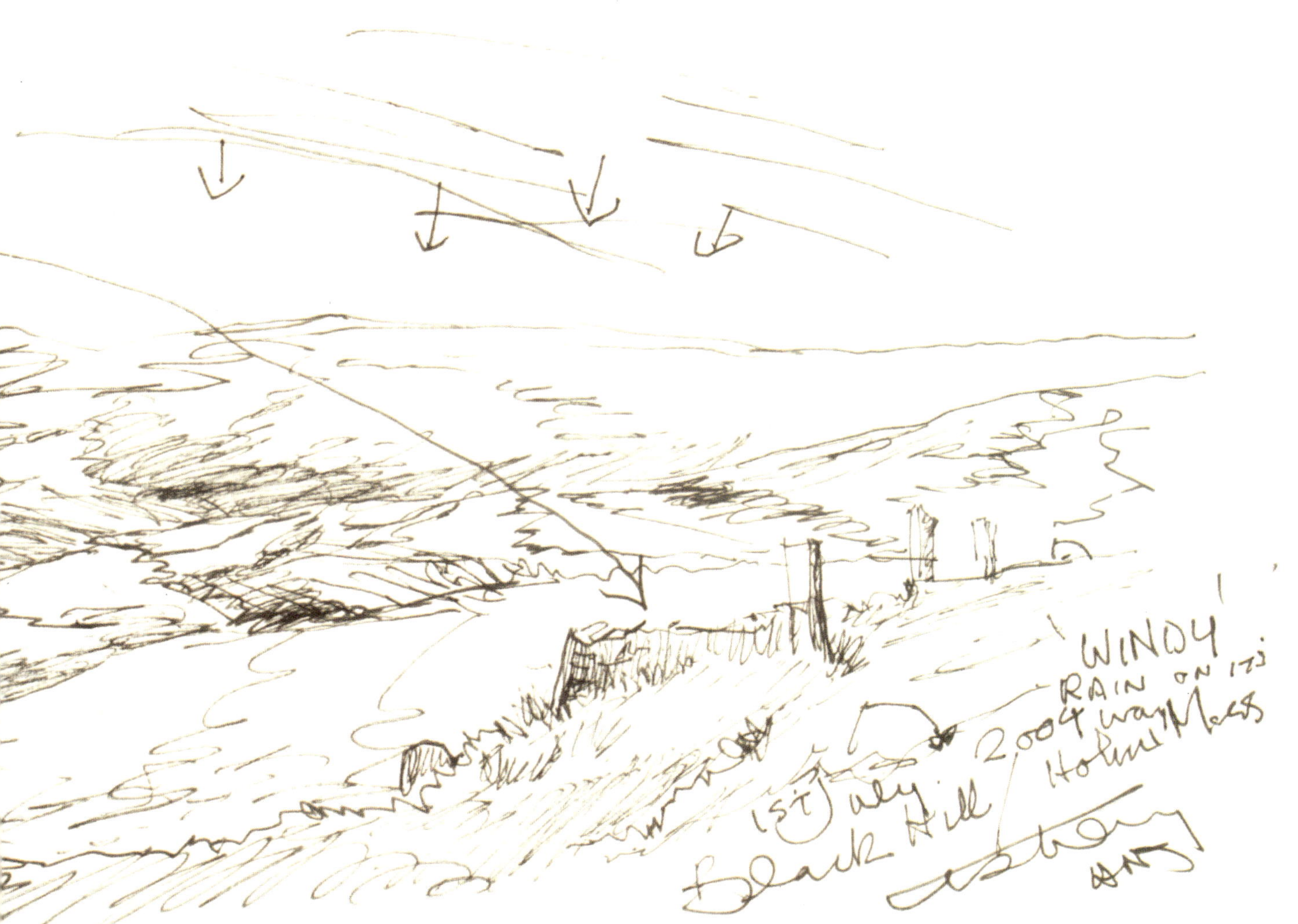
WINDY!
RAIN ON ITS way
1st July 2004
Black Hill
Holme Moss

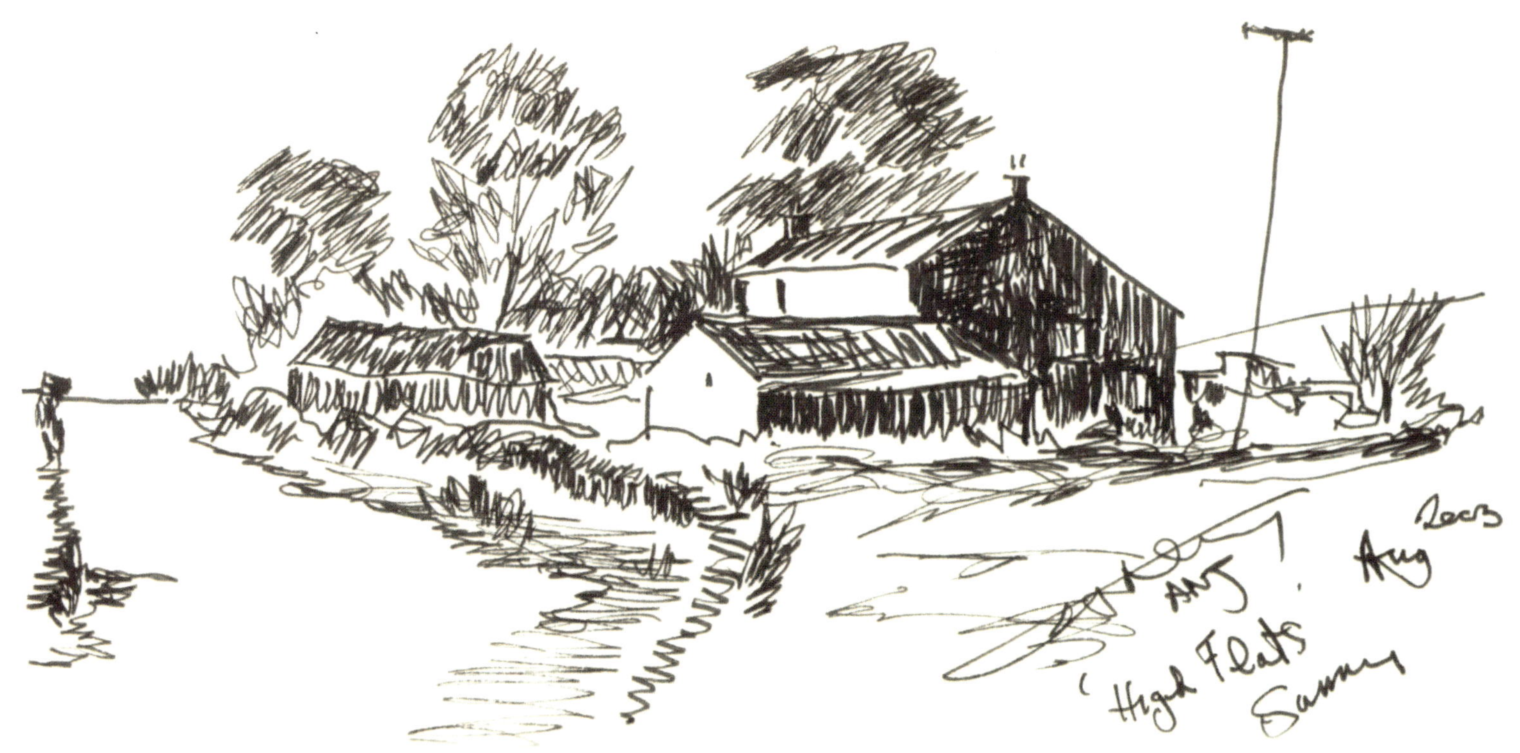
'High Flats'
Aug 2003

This is the road between Sheffield and Huddersfield.

Yorkshire has really got
a strong hold of me!
But why should I let her go
And where would I be
if she was not there..
Ashley Jackson 1970

As I reach my seventieth year I am aware of the speed at which my life has travelled. These words are from a sketchbook from 1969 and, looking back on it, it feels like only yesterday.

Carefree I go along lifes lanes and dales, seeing and feeling as I go not knowing were it will end or were there's a bend, but as I go I collect my friends.

Life must not be wasted for you only taste it but once and once only!

Years go by as fast as cats eyes on a motorway.

The art of living life is to make use of what you've got and use it to the full.

Most people don't know what they are living for, but once you have found out you have the jewel of life........

ASHLEY JACKSON 22/4/69

YORKSHIRE POST 6/6/69

he two
aces of
Yorkshire

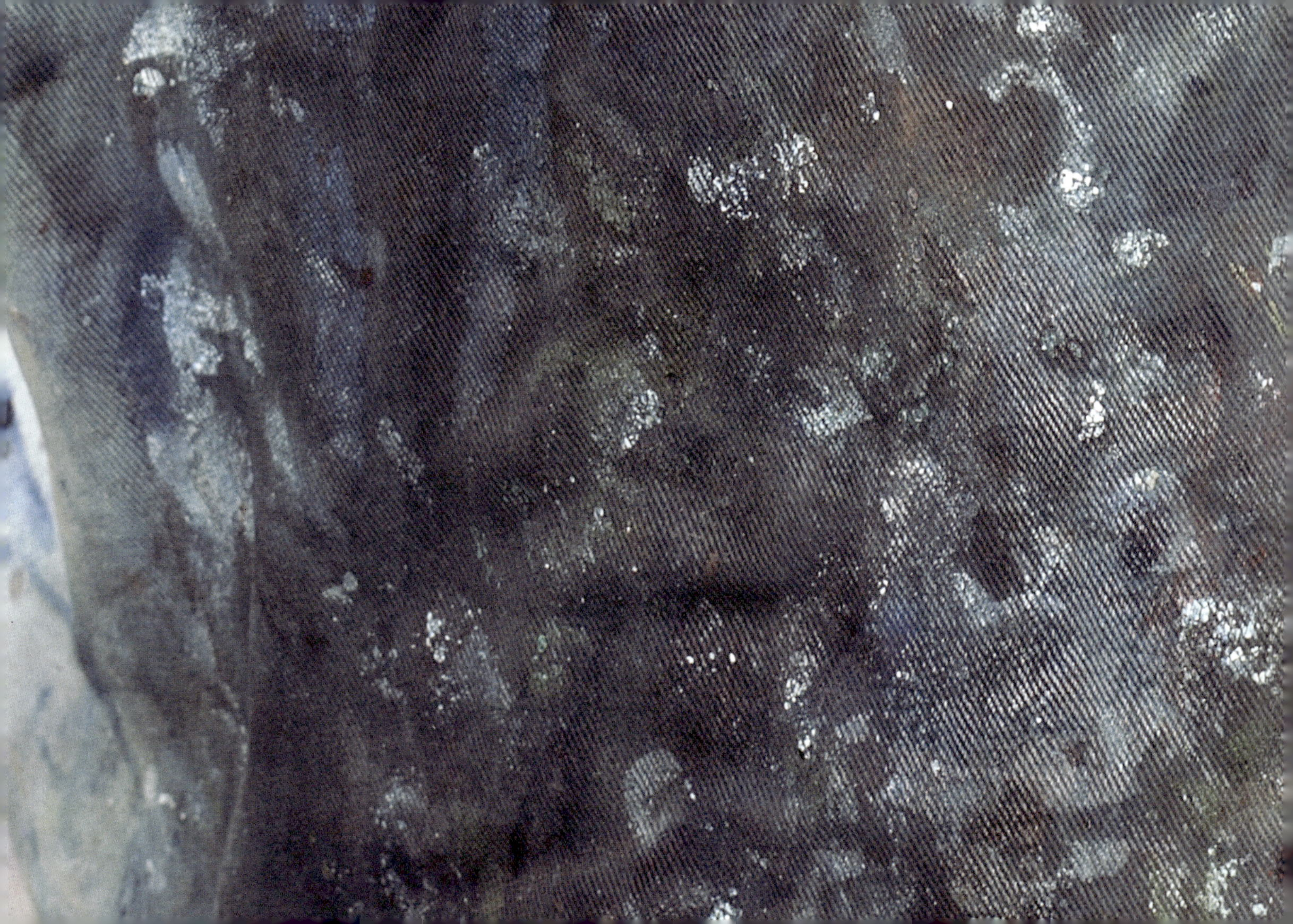